Dear Jim & Connie:

    Merry Christmas   2020

    This wonderful book, "View From My Window" is the brain child of Barbara Duriau, a french speaking Belgian living in the Netherlands.

    During the early days of the pandemic and lockdown, and when #Stay home became the global anthem, Barbara wondered what the world's population saw from its windows. The Facebook group of the same name was created by Barbara as a way for people to connect during their isolation.

    People from all four corners of the world joined the FB group. They were asked to post one photo of a view from their window. The response was overwhelming. Photos took months to be posted. From those many photos, Barbara created this book. ~~committee~~ Proceeds from sales are being donated to UNICEF's COVID relief fund.

    The photographs in this book and FB are a way to find peace and beauty in the middle of a global crisis. It's like traveling without traveling. The scenery is sometimes gorgeous, sometimes simple but all amazing, interesting and different. There are small villages, big cities, coast-lines, lakes, rivers, mountains, plains, mesas, rural areas and neighborhood streets through big and small windows. And the photos still don't capture all the beauty of this world.

    Time does not rest. When the pandemic is under control, the reunions will be glorious! But until then, enjoy this book and its views from many windows. Stay safe and well! We are all connected.

        Love,
        Pam & Pat

VIEW FROM MY WINDOW

" This group has made me realise
how beautiful our world is.
Once this pandemic stuff is over,
there are so many places on my bucket list "

- Ashley C.

Making history

View from my window is a book unlike any other.

This finely crafted work is much more than a simple compilation of photographs taken from places all over the world. It constitutes a truly exceptional first-hand account of events. This is a unique testimony to an equally unique situation. As we browse through its pages of impressive pictures, we are captivated by the astonishing encounters and moving stories it is made up of.

It is undoubtedly the first time since World War II that the common destiny of humanity is bound up with the personal destiny of each and every one of us. A virus is at the origin of this phenomenon, and its name is Covid-19.

We shall remember the Spring of 2020 for a very long time to come. Spring is the season which is traditionally associated with rebirth and light. This time, however, the days, weeks and months were filled with reports presenting alarming figures, ominous statistics and tough restrictions that infringed on our basic freedom, yet proved to be unavoidable measures.

Lockdown, tracking, confinement, preventative measures, aerosols, infectologists, experts, virologists, pandemic, epidemic, face-mask, social distancing, quarantine, cluster, hydroalcoholic gel, chloroquine. The above lexicon, which we could well have done without in our vocabulary, is a sign of the times. These words and expressions have forced their way into our everyday lives, onto our screens and media, to such an extent that many people have grown tired of always hearing and seeing them.

There is a paradox to this situation which historians, sociologists and even philosophers will confirm, namely that economic crises, ethical dilemmas, sanitary emergencies and even wars see a powerful anti-dote come to life. An amazingly fertile stimulation wells up from new awareness, leading to innovations which in normal circumstances may never have seen the light of day.

The confinement imposed by the Coronavirus pandemic has, in the same way, stimulated people's imagination and indirectly fostered creative actions which were as surprising as they were unexpected. Daring initiatives sprang up from this unusual breeding ground. How-ever, it might be pretentious of us to claim that due to the events of the year 2020, a new world is starting up and that from now on nothing will ever be quite the same again. Let's get real. We need to work a lot more together and increase global awareness before we can make this *Brave New World* possible. Nevertheless, under the strain of lockdown, people have taken the time to think and refocus on their core values, to live and consume more intelligently.

Our ability to adapt is surprising, and the artistic adventure really has no limits. Whilst the virus was following its relentless course across the planet, visual artists, singers, comedians, actors, photographers, but also ordinary citizens have discovered new ways of communicat-ing, transmitting and producing spontaneous and improvised work. As if art had suddenly become a new way of life.

Following this trend of ordinary people searching to find what is good and appealing, the social networks, which undoubtedly have never been so aptly named, will have played a considerable role, thanks to their incredible power of transmission, in creating real gems. We are invited into on-screen workshops, offices, libraries, living rooms, sitting rooms and kitchens of all kinds. Private boundaries have fad-ed and given way to unprecedented sharing. People express them-selves. Some sing, paint, write, others dance, play, have a drink, cook. We applaud and congratulate each other and exchange tips to improve our ordinary lives and make them a little more extraordinary. This cheerful patchwork of new acquaintances is inevitably based on images. This particular context triggered off the amazing adventures of the Facebook group known as *View from my window*.

Her name is **Barbara Duriau**. She is Belgian and trained as a graphic designer. She is in love with life and has the outlook of a globetrotter. Maybe this is why she could be found exercising her creative profession at the Tintin Company, home of the famous comic book hero whose adventures are characterised by his expeditions all over the world. What we can be sure of is that in her heart, she is always on the go, eager to take on new experiences. Soon after having been put in charge of the Brussels Airlines project to paint the Airbus A320 in the colours of its hero Tintin, she decided to change her life, pack her bags and leave Brussels to take off a little further north for Amsterdam.

In March 2020 with the spreading of Covid-19, a series of restrictive measures was gradually put in place in Europe and elsewhere, forcing most of the people on this planet to adopt the same behaviour, i.e. lockdown, the wearing of masks and social distancing. Barbara's Belgian and French friends shared their respective views regarding how they felt about being shut in, how they lived through it and the frustration they experienced. They also discussed new ways of coping with their fears and the reality of the situation. It is not necessarily a negative experience. Through these exchanges, Barbara envisioned a community destined to be.

It may well be a question of chance, intuition, or happy coincidence, but it was nevertheless at that time that she herself chose as the home page of her Facebook profile, a picture which was possibly prophetic. It was that of a little pink cloud set against an azure blue sky taken from a wide-open window.

Caught between the qualms and misgivings of her loved ones in isolation and her own wish to escape, an idea came to her in a flash.

We were going to be in confinement, at home with a single solitary view from our window for many long weeks. What is that view on the other side of the world? And what if I asked Internet users to take photos of their views and share them with other isolated people?

The *View from my window* Facebook group was born.

Its birth certificate dates from **March 22nd 2020**. A window on the world opened. March 23rd Barbara posted and shared her view from her studio in Amsterdam. **344** people accepted her invitation. The following day there were **2,675**. One week later, **50,000**! April 15th **one million**!

On April 26th the *View from my window* Facebook group had more than **two million members**.

When the project went viral, the international press got hold of it and was delighted to tell a happy story at such a gloomy moment in time. The founder gave interviews about her group, which was now considered as a social phenomenon. Internet users of many countries, including Belgium, The Netherlands, France, Italy, Greece, Hungary, Portugal, the United Kingdom, Vietnam, the United States, New Zealand, Mali, along with the international print media and online press, all wanted to know a little more about this success story that began at the dawn of a springtime unlike any other.

The richness of *View from my window* is to be found in its wealth of multiple contrasting views posted by members of the group. A real community has grown over these past months, built on solidarity, exchanges and tokens of friendship. This book has become its family album and pays homage to that community. Humanity is celebrated here in the best light it can possibly offer through its anecdotes, its testimonies and its relevant pictures.

📍 Amsterdam | The Netherlands | March 26 2020 | 7:53 pm

Barbara's home office. A small desk, a small window, a big story!

Meet Barbara Duriau

| Founder of *View from my window* |

Original text by **Dominique Maricq** 📍 Rixensart, Belgium | 29th July 2020

— What were the guidelines for posting a photo to your group?
The idea was very simple. You had to take a photo of the view from your own home, either from your window or your balcony and then share it with the group.

— Did you have to establish ground rules for photos to appear in this group?
Yes, it was crucial in order to prevent members from posting inappropriate content that would go against the community's philosophy. Take, for example, close-ups of pets or flowers, multiple or panoramic photos, videos, people you could clearly identify, photos of people with their feet up or having evening drinks. The goal was really to capture the moment in all its simplicity, with an emphasis on the view itself.

— It seems to me that the people you know quickly passed on the information. Do you have any idea how this bubble grew?
Two days after creating the group, I asked a friend who lives in Miami to invite her Facebook friends to join the group. That was already a huge opening on the world!

— The transition to global went pretty fast...
Very fast indeed! We shared information thanks to via-via, through acquaintances from either Australia or South Africa. So, the movement went global thanks to a few connections from my small network. I never imagined that it was going to take off in the way it did.

Of course, I was expecting a certain amount of success, considering how much free time the population had following lockdown, and I un-

derstood the escapism that we all frankly yearned for. But I never ex-
pected a craze like that, involving more than over 2 million members.

— **When were you absolutely convinced that something incredible
was happening?**
When the group reached 100,000 people, and during my first interview
on April 4th on Belgian national radio, RTBF (Vivacité), followed by a TV
appearance on RTL-TVI. Subsequently, the international press became
interested in VFMW. *Le Figaro*, CBS, *Livemint*, ABC, *Huffingtonpost* Japan,
BBC News Vietnam, to name but a few examples.

— **So for you, was there a real before and after VFMW?**
For sure! A big professional project fell through at the start of lockdown, so I was wondering about my future.

Then Sunday, March 22nd was the day I envisioned the group. The next
day, March 23rd, it was online. From that day on, my life changed completely. I don't think coming up with the idea and designing *View from my
window* was entirely fortuitous. It brings together all the things that I love
and makes my life exciting: the images, the graphics through the creation of the logo and the cover that I change daily. We could also add my
passion for travel, sharing it with others and making new connections.

— Is there a typical day for you as the head administrator of the group?
My timetable is scheduled like a crazy clock. For the first few months, as soon as I woke up, I would open up the group and I'd be really curious to check out the new posts, whilst also bearing in mind the rules that I had established. It was just a question then of moderating the group by deleting certain topics that would go against the rules of good behaviour, and by tempering controversies on issues of a political and ideological nature, for example, people for or against Trump. I had to deal with the jealousy of some individuals as well. Then, I would choose the photo of the day that would illustrate the cover of the group. Finally, I would approve some pending posts.

Requests for interviews followed, which took up a bit of my time and added another layer of stress as most were in English, which is not my first language.

— When did you transition from being a single creator to the role of team leader?
Two days after the launch of *View from my window*, I asked my sister Catherine to help me. She often tells me that she recalls that particular moment so well it seems to be etched in her mind. By then, there were 2,000 members, and the photos were already arriving so quickly that it was impossible for me to keep up. Then, close friends agreed to help me out. Given the circumstances, they had free time and got caught up in the game. It was an addictive game, which I refrained from warning them about!

I also relied on a few moderators from Texas. Even though my nights were short, this collaboration coming straight from the US enabled me to handle posts that were being transmitted to me while I slept. Due to the time difference, these helping hands were necessary to keep up the pace. All in all, dozens of people found themselves at their laptops, and, depending on their time schedules, sometimes as administrators or moderators of the group. They were all volunteers!

— Were certain decisions difficult to make?

April 29th was a key date. Many countries, including Belgium, were starting to lift the lockdown measures. From then on, we really wanted to prevent members from posting pictures taken from places other than their homes, like their workplace, for example. Let's not lose sight of the fact that it was about showing the impact of the lockdown on everyone's daily life. I wanted to remain true to this basic concept.

Our decision was reinforced by the incredible success of the group. We were faced with a phenomenon that constantly kept growing. An exponential curve that didn't show any signs of falling. It could have become unmanageable, even with a reinforcement of the team. Ten photos would arrive when we were busy processing just one. So, I decided not to accept new members and therefore new photos. On the other hand, it was obvious that we were going to continue to process the thousands of pending posts, more than 200,000, in fact!

By refusing new posts starting from April 29th, I knew I was going to disappoint thousands of people. But, I knew this was the right thing to do. The intention was not to end up in the record books by being the biggest group on Facebook. That was not my goal at all.

— Were there any major technical problems?

Yes, as surprising as it sounds, it was the Facebook bugs. An issue with the actual timeline caused a lot of upset within the community. They didn't understand what was going on behind the scenes.

What was also quite stressful was that we couldn't see the number of photos pending for approval. Were there 50,000 left? 100,000? 300,000? It was sometimes disheartening to work in the dark. Finally, we had a big incident in July. A student who lacked knowledge on the workings of a Facebook group, changed the group's setting to *private*, which, up to this point, had been *public*! Seven hours of talks and discussions with Facebook engineers were needed to resolve the issue. I had to journey my way through the highest Facebook ranks to finally be able to click on that infamous button, which I had never had access to, by the way, to '*free up*' VFMW and bring it back to its original status!

— Did you ever anticipate the consequences of managing such a group?
This has been a very satisfying experience and has brought me unexpected gratitude and moments of intense and exhilarating happiness. I realised the group brought me a real breath of fresh air.

We called it *The Feel-Good Group*. I can add to that the thousands of positive comments, and the touching messages that I have received* in relation to how beneficial this community was. On the other hand, it was also highly stressful.

From the moment I woke up to the moment I went to bed, it was as if I were on permanent duty. I had to deal with concerns related to bugs, conflicts between members, remembering to delete comments under posts that might take a hateful turn. Fortunately, I had the support of my internal team, who demonstrated unprecedented efficiency and moral support. I cannot thank them enough! Trusting them, learning to delegate, those were things that I had never done in my life before.

— At a critical moment, you wrote and published a very poignant open letter entitled *I was not ready*. Could you explain the reason behind this?
I really needed to do that. It had been coming to a head for a while. I was getting angrier and angrier and was close to burnout. One day, I completely broke down, just like in the movies, except that in this case, it wasn't play-acting but for real. That's when I said to myself; I have to write. I need to make myself heard to show that I am a real human being with my own emotions, not some robot behind this group, and that sometimes I have a hard time dealing with haters. I also had to deal with the numerous copycat groups, which sprang up like poisonous mushrooms.

This was also when I decided to launch crowdfunding to infuse a second life into *View from my window*. I knew that this announcement was going to unleash all kinds of feelings and reactions, good, not so good, even downright insulting. Some members imagined that all of this came from a strong drive to make money, that this group was all about profit, and that somehow, I was taking advantage of a difficult time and exploiting a distressful situation. I most emphatically reject these allegations.

— **It seems that the creation of VFMW taught you a lot about yourself, your capacity for resilience but also your limits.**
Before I posted the open letter, a friend of mine stated: *"But you wanted this lifestyle!"* I answered, NO, I did not. At first, I was only focused on the group, but then this new life quickly overwhelmed me.

I have often imagined returning to the person I was before, with a quiet life and no particular worries except for the uncertainty of the future. I wanted to give up everything but I couldn't, I couldn't allow myself to do that.

It's only much later that I realised that I could see things through. Friends would say to me, *"You should stop, take a break."* I just couldn't because I knew that this group depended mostly on me. It was a huge responsibility. With hindsight, I recognise how strong I was at that time, although in the heat of the moment, I never told myself to be strong. As far as I was concerned, I simply needed to continue the amazing adventure that I had started. I had this image of myself, trapped in a high-speed train, with no brakes, that would one day crash into a marshmallow mountain.

— **You almost created a job without realising it?**
It was a double full-time job. I've never worked so much in my life! I would usually work fifteen hours a day, weekends included. I took a single day off during the four months of managing the group. I remember one day, a friend asked me a question. It was probably *the* question they should never have asked me. (laughs): *"So what are you up to now? Found a job yet?"* I answered, maybe a little too sharply: *"View from my window is my job!"* A voluntary unpaid job.

— **Were there any posts that particularly moved you?**

So many of them! There are those that make me shiver and bring tears to my eyes and others that make me smile again when the work gets too repetitive.

I'll mention just one story, that of my Belgian-American friend Sonja, also an administrator, who wrote on our WhatsApp group: *"Ok, sorry girls, if this does nothing for you, but for me, I swear I just had goosebumps and my heart started beating faster... so I just approved a photo... of the small town where I was born 47 years ago, deep in the heart of the United States... Pittsfield, Massachusetts... I am quite overwhelmed... to know that a guy from way over there posted his little photo and the fact that by sheer chance I fell upon it and I had to approve it. Now that really chokes you up!"*

In the end, this is one of the extremely positive sides of social media. VFMW has allowed members to rekindle old friendships they'd lost sight of for several years because they'd moved to another continent for example. This group has truly been a great human adventure. Everything about *View from my window* has really moved me.

This group has truly been a great human adventure. Everything about *View from my window* has really moved me.

*I would like to apologise for the thousands of private messages I received that I was unable to reply to!

View from my window

Time has stood still.
We no longer see things the same way.

The window is wide open; we are attentive to the world's heartbeat.
We look out upon a scene of everyday life that appears frozen in time.

Our street has become a small theatre, and on its stage, a few bit players are hurrying to get home. The sound of silence has taken over, playing its part in a strange and rare ritual, that of a world reduced to its simplest form.

We used to hear, now we listen. We used to see, now we watch. Minute details suddenly stand out and what is ordinary becomes quite extraordinary.

The window is both air and light.
Whether it slides, pivots or swivels, it is a framework defining our living environment.
It is high or low, round or oval, square or oblong.
Its shape influences how we perceive and its outline determines how we consider the view, *our own* view.
We feel that this link with the outside world is now more important than ever.
Sometimes our eyes stray well beyond the horizon.

We long for that *elsewhere*, but it is in the here and now that things are happening.

Through a sheer net curtain, a half-open shutter or the slats of a louvred shutter, we can observe endless versions of a living picture in colour.
It is the view from our window.

Sandra Vivier 📍 Brussels | Belgium | April 4 | 3:00 pm

Leena Klossner 📍 Hämeenlinna | Finland | April 10 | 7:15 am

Maria Tran 📍 Olympic Valley, California | USA | April 6 | 6:54 am

Sunrise after a big snowstorm. This view provides me solace in these difficult times. The past few nights, we've turned off all the lights to take in the night skies. It forces us to turn off the devices, turn away from the news and spend some quiet time before we go to bed.

Guido Carlo Alleva 📍 Grazzano Badoglio, Asti | Italy | April 1 | 6:00 pm

Christine Lucas 📍 Rio de Janeiro | Brazil | April 28 | 12:00 pm

Hi everyone! I bring here another reality, despite so many beautiful views I've seen around. I just have a boring sight from the inner block but I still get a good amount of sunlight and breeze I can't complain at all. I'm happy and grateful in my home. Stay well!

Alexa Sokol 📍 Belgrade | Serbia | April 4 | 2:57 pm

Anastasia Venetsanou 📍 Oia Santorini | Greece | April 17 | 10:49 am

Until today there is no Covid-19 case in the island and the spring is wonderful here.

Lili Bach 📍 Annaberg | Austria | April 7 | 5:05 pm

Day 28 of lockdown. Almost a month that I've seen my mom. I buy her groceries which are being brought to her apartment since we are not allowed into the residential complex and we talk on the phone every day. But it's not the same. No hugs. At the age of 89 it's hard for her to understand what's going on. And it must be disturbing, yes, frightening. Not to know if you will live long enough to ever go outside again.

No idea when school will start again for my 16 year old son or how grades for the annual report will be determined. My husband is a great and dedicated tour guide travelling the world eight months of the year. Well, not this year. (Love you Vernon Howard!!)

Yet we are so immensely grateful to have each other and to have this view. A lake in total isolation. Only lots of robins, titmouses, ducks and herons make their cheerful music, sheeps mowing gently in the distance and a squirrel visits every morning. This is as good as it gets. It's just a home away from home for one week. Home is Vienna, Austria. Looking out into the world these days we are still blessed, not only to have this view. Very thankful for that! Keep up your good spirit and stay healthy!

Tania Shah 📍 Mumbai | India | April 12 | 11:52 am

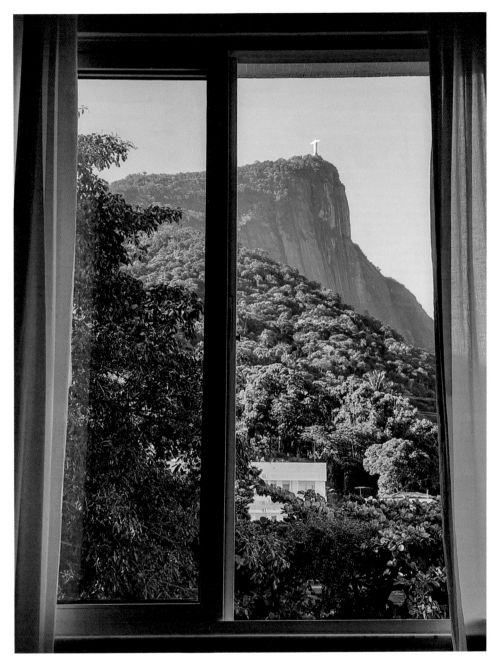

Lu Fraga 📍 Rio de Janeiro | Brazil | April 26 | 12:17 pm

Gina Cooper 📍 Atlanta, Georgia | USA | April 14 | 3:13 pm

Sue Stanford 📍 Hollywood, California | USA | April 22 | 2:22 pm

I live in the heart of Hollywood California. This building was built in 1929 by Paramount Studios and housed some of its stars. I can see as far as 12 miles from my window.

Siwla Silva 📍 Paraibuna | Brazil | April 28 | 4:19 pm

Mask making with a view.

Madeleine Eno 📍 Sandy, Oregon | USA | April 13 | 8:26 am

Matisse Andersen Gympie, Sunshine Coast | Australia | April 11 | 2:04 pm

Elizabeth Simpson New Orleans, Louisiana | USA | April 28 | 6:25 pm

I overlook the courtyards from the early 19th century, magnolias and palms. I hear a fountain down below and smell jasmine and ginger. It is my happy place - thinking of you in yours and send love.

Steve Jakobs 📍 Brussels | Belgium | March 30 | 12:19 pm

Mattia Baseggio 📍 Venice | Italy | March 29 | 6:14 pm

Mark Minkevitch 📍 Friday Harbor, Washington | USA | April 28 | 5:11 am

Kaisa Kauppinen Li | Finland | April 11 | 9:41 pm

Michel Vaerewijck Antwerp | Belgium | March 30 | 2:58 pm

My small office & library. Rear view from our 1923 ter-
raced cottage house, in the city outskirts. This room used
to be the baby room of my daughter, a dressing of my
grandparents, and before that my fathers children's bedroom, etc...

My daughter is the fifth consecutive generation in this
house, that was bought by my great-grandfather just before the Great Depression (that cost him a bankruptcy, his
health and life). My grandad lived here with his new bride
and mother during WW2 and had their son while allied
bombers dropped bombs and were getting piled by the
next door Flak battery. Shaking the house a little more,
V1's fell around at the end of the war. Cracks in the walls
are a witness to the many different crisis this house has
sheltered my ancestors from.

After many decades of tranquility it is our turn to sit this
one out and hope for the best. Take care all, and stay safe!.

Zrinka Raguž 📍 Dubrovnik | Croatia | April 18 | 8:30 am

Alice Visscher 📍 Fenn, Alberta | Canada | April 1 | 11:44 am

Marina Hayes 📍 New York City, New York | USA | April 14 | 6:30 am

Kinta Chuc 📍 Aosta Valley | Italy | April 8 | 10:39 am

Paige M 📍 Priest River, Idaho | USA | April 23 | 7:19 pm

While it looks still and serene, much is happening. Snow still melting, geese nesting, deer grazing, the occasional bunny passes by, birds of every make and model, and so much wild that I can't describe it. You know when the air feels different and how it makes you want to take deep breaths? That's how it feels at this view from my window.

Els de Haas ♥ Dordrecht | The Netherlands | March 31 | 5:15 pm

Anne Pflimlin ♀ London | United Kingdom | April 10 | 10:30 am

Connor Stewie 📍 Brooklyn, New York | USA | April 15 | 8:17 pm

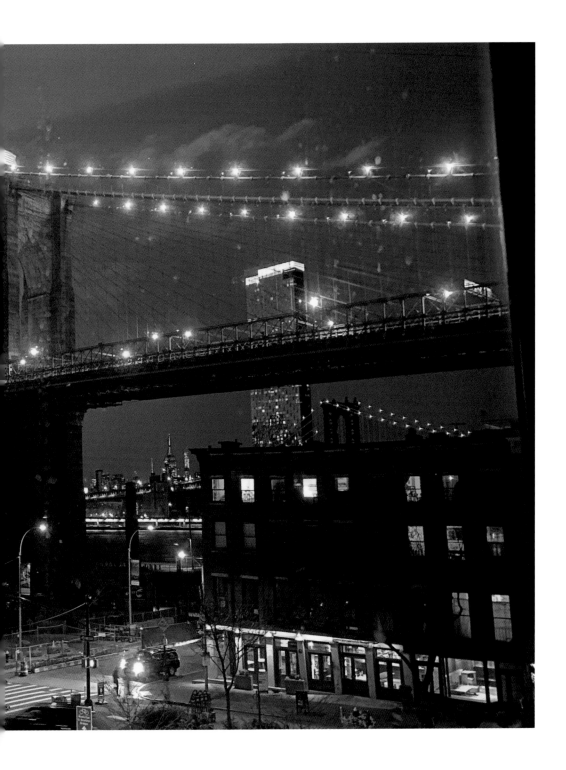

Merja Anttila 📍 Oulujärvi | Finland | April 13 | 12:28 pm

Aurelie Hox Brussels | Belgium | April 3 | 12:55 pm

Maria Birnaure 📍 Bucharest | Romania | April 28 | 7:50 pm

We should all be grateful that we have the chance to see another day ending. For these days to last until we're old, we must stay healthy, especially during this hard times! Wishing you all a long life full of outstanding days! Me, my fiancee and our cat are very lucky to live in a new area of the city, surrounded by green fields and houses, as we are nature lovers and we miss trips and walks a lot. The view we have from our apartment gives us the faith that we will soon be able to taste the sweet perfume of nature again.

Angela Gualanduzzi 📍 Bologna | Italy | April 10 | 11:30 am

I live in the historical centre of Bologna and the oval window in my bedroom offers a view that sums up the typical elements of Bolognese architecture, namely the tiled roofs of the buildings, the *altane*, the rooftop terraces, the yellow, red and pink facades of the houses.

Molly Bohman 📍 Bigfork, Montana | USA | April 25 | 8:13 am

Mike Escober 📍 Calabanga Camarines Sur | Philippines | April 26 | 10:23 am

On our 43rd day of Enhanced Community Quarantine LOCKDOWN, a well spent breezy summertime in our farmhouse overlooking herbs, veggies, and fruiting plants.

Necla sarikaya 📍 Bozeman, Montana | USA | April 12 | 11:00 am

This corner in my house I sit and relax by drinking Turkish tea or coffee with my dog Teddy.

Deserted streets

A solitary tram, all lights ablaze, makes its way across the deserted streets.
The heartbeat of the city has slowed down. Unusual sounds fill the squares.
There's a kind of hush over the scene, and a fragrant perfume hangs in the air.
All around, life awaits with bated breath; the stones remain mute.
Silence reigns supreme.

The far-away wailing of an ambulance.
Grim headlines dominate the news.

Life, discreet and barely visible, is still perceptible and well and truly there.
On the main thoroughfares, the constant comings and goings of vehicles
is now a distant memory.
Pedestrians, few and far between, occupy the streets, taken aback by such
freedom of movement.
Cycles whizz gaily down the wide avenues now empty of cars, buses and trucks.

Boulevards have lost their original purpose.
The buildings on either side of them, be they impressive manor houses
or soulless apartment buildings, stand like majestic sentinels, now deprived
of the bustling activity they usually keep watch over.

Nothing is the same. Everything is different.

Town and country are united in the same fate by an invisible line.
The common denominator of another universe.
The deserted streets are an unprecedented hiatus in this new millennium.

Ernesto Fernandes Rosa Neto ● São Paulo | Brazil | March 22 | 6:40 pm

Kira Milas 📍 Amsterdam | The Netherlands | April 8 | 7:36 pm

Canals are closed to boats and it's unusually (and pleasantly) quiet.

Jlizée Aouffroy 📍 Brussels | Belgium | April 6 | 6:04 pm

Can you see the Atomium?

Elektra Samoili ⚑ Paris | France | April 25 | 7:00 am

Place de l'Hôtel de Ville from our living room, windows open to the morning breeze, my pianist husband giving a concert for the pigeons social distancing in the square.

Peter Sinkovics 📍 Budapest | Hungary | April 22 | 8:46 pm

No people, no cars, a temporary bicycle lane and an empty tram.

Sabina Ragaini 📍 Venice | Italy | March 19 | 4:00 pm

The city is empty, silent, beautiful, amazing and sad. We are all at home and we go out only for buying food, like in other towns in Italy. Birds and fishes live their freedom.

Be careful all of you, do not read too much news about us abroad, we are at home and this is the best way to protect yourself. Do not long to see your children if they were studying abroad, they are the main 'transport' for the virus and they can very easily bring the virus to old people in the family. Be good and be safe!

Peter Morgan 📍 Denver, Colorado | USA | April 15 | 9:37 am

Yilin 📍 Kuala Lumpur | Malaysia | April 11 | 12:00 am

I live in concrete jungle, where city development is rapid & massive, with few major highways lined within different residential & commercial areas. Today marks the 26th day of Malaysia's Movement Control Order. We see clearer sky, cleaner river, air feels fresher and way less traffic pollution. It seems like mother earth has been taking a short break from us.

Giusy Di Nardo 📍 Bellona | Italy | April 28 | 2:26 pm

Tammy D. Switzer 📍 Santa Fe, New Mexico | USA | April 13 | 10:04 am

Leslie Pierce 📍 Utqiagvik, Alaska | USA | April 26 | 10:07 am

12 °F . 22 mph / 35 kph winds from the West. Just another spring day at the Top of the World!

Φανή Γιαλαμά 📍 Nafplion | Greece | April 1 | 3:00 pm

Manuela Restagno 📍 Milan | Italy | March 20 | 5.39 pm

Walter Rodrigues 📍 New York City, New York | USA | April 4 | 12:59 pm

This is the view from my apartment, looking over Rockefeller Center NYC. What is usually one of the most active and visited landmarks in New York City, became a startling, desolate view for months. This city has never experienced such silence and eerie tranquility. I hope that we never again have to endure the suffering and tragedy that surrounded the city that I love.

Oneida Ann Murphy 📍 Destin, Florida | USA | April 26 | 9:00 am

Boo Gee Soo 📍 Singapore | April 5 | 8:00 am

82 degrees Fahrenheit. Humid.

This is view from home, stuck here at level 23 little apartment, this is day 7 of "circuit breaker" period, in general people follow rules here. Hopefully we could keep the virus at the bay in 2 more weeks.

Overseeing here is the Causeway, the bridge that connects us and Malaysia, is peacefully resting compared to it's usual hectic mode.

Across the bridge is where my parents live. Miss ya dada & mama although we talk on the phone everyday. When I see them after the pandemic, promise, going to hug them real tight!

Let us stay United and keep fighting! Sending love from Singapore!

Fernando García-Bastidas 📍 Wageningen | The Netherlands | April 4 | 10:59 pm

Michelle Rodiger ♥ Brisbane, Queensland | Australia | April 21 | 6:43 pm

This hasn't got a filter on it - just the way the street lights turned out. Our little street is a lot quieter these days. Stay safe everyone. We're all in this together.

May Agius 📍 Sliema | Malta | April 12 | 3:04 pm

Juan David Mejia 📍 Aventura, Florida | USA | April 14 | 7:31 pm

A clear view from my balcony without cruises at the horizon, no boats on the waterways, no airplanes... Blessings!

Mieke Verkeyn 📍 Lodi | Italy | April 26 | 2:30 pm

This is obviously not Lodi in California, but the capital of the small province also called Lodi in Northern Italy where the first Covid-19 cases in Europe were diagnosed. It's unusually quiet here these days, but the historic buildings (on the right the Cathedral and the town hall and in the centre-left the Incoronata church which is especially lovely on the inside) make me realise that the town will survive this very sad episode in history.

To the left is actually one of the most beautiful squares in Italy. It is arcaded on all four sides and covered in pebbles that were sourced from the river nearby (it is further than 200 metres away so I cannot go there these days, but rather than 200 metres, I can't wait to travel 1000 km to visit my family in Belgium!). Unfortunately the nicest building on the other side is currently covered up and there's a crane dominating the view; work in progress, or better: since several weeks the works are on hold, waiting for better times, which will hopefully come soon!

Carmen A. Leguia 📍 Lima | Peru | April 10 | 12:55 pm

Gaetano Balestra 📍 Naples | Italy | April 10 | 9:00 am

The view from my window in the typical Neapolitan street, the "Vico", usually full of life, but now so empty for the emergency... and so, best greetings to everyone, stay safe and everything will be fine.

Alexandra Lee Cola 📍 Manhattan, New York | USA | April 19 | 11:28 am

From our balcony... 31st Floor on 3rd Ave.
Looking at 3rd Ave so empty. But it comes alive @ 7 PM everyday for a min or 2, people make all kinds of noise as a way of thanking all frontliners. GOD bless us all.

Yamini Lila Kumar 📍 Florence | Italy | April 27 | 7:48 pm

All you need is love

Love is universal.
It unites nations and peoples.

Love can be taken or given and can be tempered.
Love is contagious. You can let love in and send love out regardless of borders,
fences and walls, no matter how high they may be.
We need it all around us like the healing qualities of soothing ointments which
penetrate and cure the wounds of the body and soul.

Words scrawled in chalk on grounds of concrete.
Banners flapping in the wind.
Writings on the wall, in the true Dazibao tradition.
Little notes stuck to window panes.
Welcoming wreaths of flowers.
Flags flying for nations or for prayers.
Graffiti as beautiful as old masters.

The whys and wherefores do not matter; what really matters is the
determination to keep the banner of love flying high.

We share, we give, we receive, we help, we listen, and we commit to one another.
Love shows itself. It is in our eyes and at our fingertips. It is on our window sills.

Billboard signs turn into cheerful messages.
In an apartment building, windows light up here and there.
They turn into the shape of a giant heart.
No need to explain, there is power in the symbol.

Infinite goodness is there, and we came face to face with it.

Melanie Smith 📍 Brisbane, Queensland | Australia | April 17 | 10:00 am

My girlfriend flew out from London last year to help me through cancer treatment. It's my second bout with breast cancer and the second time she has flown halfway round the world to look after me! She planted this growing wall for me and I'm grateful every day for blue skies and good friends and a safe warm home to recover in.

Patricia Michelle 📍 Atlanta, Georgia | USA | April 28 | 8:30 pm

At the end of the street... a heart to support all the doctors and nurses.

Masako Matsumoto 📍 Kashiwa, Chiba | Japan | April 22 | 10:00 am

I am a Japanese native, living in Kashiwa, Chiba in the sub-urbs of Tokyo. (1 hour by train to go to the office in Tokyo). We, all the employees at company, is currently working remotely from home, past 8 weeks. Sometimes I bring my PC on the garden table and work outside.

I live with handicapped mom, 90 years old, taking care of her over 20 years. Until recently, I was frustrated spending 24/7 with her but in other way of thinking, I found there are many moms and daughters and families who can't see each other for a long time. Now, I'm just thankful in being able to spend a day like today, and try to think it's a good chance to do my best for her. I also feel so grateful for her caregiver, visiting her 2 hours a day, 4 times a week even in this hard time. I appreciate all the people who work front line, at this turbulent times.

"When 'I' is replaced with 'We,'
even "illness" becomes "wellness.""

This quote has been meaningful to me... and now more than ever "we" can apply it to help those around us, in staying at home.

Sending love from Japan. Take care, everyone.

*Added by Masako Mastsumoto

All the heartfelt comments and messages around the world they all became my precious treasure. Replying to the comments and direct messages one by one was a hard work, it took two weeks to finish all of them was a hard work for me, but that makes me smiles and tears... feeling we are not alone... and appreciated the time I could spent "connecting".

Tom De Coninck 📍 Roeselare | Belgium | April 1 | 6:45 pm

Carol Kafton 📍 Portland, Oregon | USA | April 2 | 7:00 pm

This view is not the prettiest, but is the one that makes my heart sing. From my kitchen window I see across my driveway to my neighbor's kitchen window. We have lived across from each other for over 40 years, and through these windows, have shared life's joys (weddings, births...) and life's sadnesses (deaths, divorces...). For my 60th birthday, she gave me the the picture above the window she had made for me. You can see it if you scroll in – "May you always be at the window." This is my favorite window.

Marcela Drumm 📍 Düsseldorf | Germany | April 10 | 9:00 am

Terry Schwartz 📍 Topeka, Kansas | USA | April 11 | 10:14 am

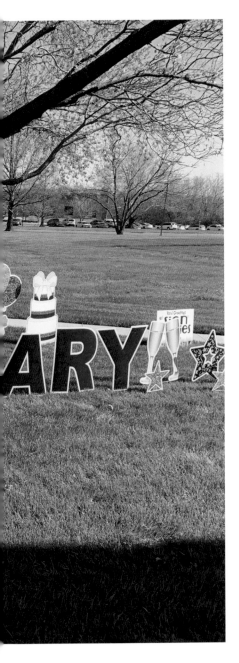

This isn't the view from MY window, but from my in-laws' window at their assisted living home. Reaching 70 years of marriage is amazing and we couldn't let it pass without a celebration – no parties in these trying times – but we found a way to honor them!

As all assisted living places are on complete lockdown, I took this photo in front of their window and then used my cell phone to call them inside. They were so surprised and the smiles on their faces were priceless!

Tom Herrmann 📍 Montreal, Québec | Canada | April 24 | 3:15 pm

Here's the view from my window in beautiful Montreal, Quebec, Canada, where it's not quite spring yet! Many people on our street have decorated their homes with rainbows and the message "Ça va bien aller" or "It will all be OK". In this strange period of social distancing, I am humbled how much the world has come together to protect those most vulnerable to catching this disease. Wherever you are, remember: we may be separated now, but this is an unprecedented showing of humans coming together to help one another.

Shelley Lewis 📍 Sidney, British Columbia | Canada | April 28 | 9:00 am

From my dining room window. I am in a high risk group so I have to be very mindful, I fly all country flags as prayer flags in my front yard. Blessings to this wonderful planet that we all call home! Be safe!

Rebecca Ellen 📍 Chicago, Illinois | USA | April 26 | 10:58 am

This is my view out at the South Loop. Our neighborhood is filled with signs and symbols of hope and love and solidarity. I am filled with the same, especially being so lucky to be quarantined with a wonderful man who asked me to marry him and posted the response in post-its on our window. I'm sending out Aloha and would love to hear back your own stories of small and large happy moments during this difficult time.

Sue Soutor 📍 Mesa, Arizona | USA | April 2 | 10:30 am

Laura Reid 📍 Barrie, Ontario | Canada | April 21 | 8:00 am

We bought this condo overlooking Lake Simcoe just before our province declared a state of emergency. Then my American husband and daughter raced off to DC to clear out her dorm room. They've opted to stay in the US until the situation stabilizes. I have almost no furniture, but no curtains means I can always see this serenity. I have a 9 year-old black pom who is good company.

When we take our walks on the waterfront, I distribute sandwiches to the homeless. Even they know about social distancing. I have developed a pretty good right hand toss. But I'm not going to lie: when this first started, I was optimistic that I could handle it well. But I am starting to feel like that John Prine song, *Hello in There*.

Stephanie Clarke 📍 Medford, Oregon | USA | April 17 | 6:53 am

I am British and was living in Johannesburg, S. Africa until Covid19 rocked my world - in a good way. I took this photo today from my new home in Medford, Oregon, USA.

The date is 21 April, 2020. My American fiance and I are celebrating our 10-month anniversary today. We met in the Great Pyramid in Egypt last June. Our wedding was planned for 25 April in S. Africa.

When the travel restrictions started and my fiance's flight to S. Africa was cancelled, we made an overnight decision that I would fly to America before the US borders closed too. One week later, on 23 March, I got one of the last 2 seats on the last flight out of Johannesburg to the USA.

We had always planned to write a book about our amazing relationship and now the title: "Love in the time of the Corona Virus" seems apropos. Thank you everyone for your glorious posts on Facebook. They make my soul sing.

Rikki Jones 📍 Chicago, Illinois | USA | April 16 | 8:54 pm

Animal kingdom

Our pets are here, right next to us.
Over there are other animals, the so-called wild ones.

They all, each and every one of them, follow their instinct, quite unaware
of these extraordinary world events.

Proud, free and independent, they roam through a magical garden
and under an arch of peace.
They are the kings of the world.

We meet them in strange and unexpected circumstances.
There is a sense of trust and companionship in the air.
Curiosity, fear and tenderness too.
Who is the more surprised of the two? Man or beast?

An astonishing parade of animals with their furs, skins, fleeces and feathers
comes towards our homes. Their territory and ours seem to merge together.

So near and yet so far away.

Jennifer Aungelique 📍 Wasilla, Alaska | USA | April 1 | 1:50 pm

Helen Atherton Kyneton, Victoria | Australia | April 20 | 6:46 pm

Kestell Serfontein 📍 Stellenbosch | South Africa | April 10 | 3:59 pm

Deon Meyer 📍 Kachikau | Botswana | April 9 | 7:30 am

I am a wildlife guide in South Africa and Botswana, where we are privileged to live with free wildlife animals. Like most of the world we are locked down with only essential services allowed to continue. But outside my window and my porch life goes on, like it did for millions of years on the plains of Africa. Please stay safe.

Shena Louise 📍 South Killingholme | United Kingdom | April 15 | 5:00 pm

The view from my bedroom window of my Animal Sanctuary. We look after 160 animals, many disabled and terminally ill.

Cynthia Gutierrez-White 📍 Reisterstown, Maryland | USA | March 31 | 12:31 pm

We moved here before the stay-at-home mandate - Mawas enacted. Settling in has been a wonderful distraction for the whole family. Haley, here, is the most vigilant of all our dogs. She's constantly guarding us from raccoons, deer and foxes. Be safe, everyone!

Stuart McKelvie 📍 Canmore, Alberta | Canada | March 19 | 8:43 am

Town has become so quiet, the animals have started checking on us to make sure we're doing okay. Stay happy, healthy, and home everybody!

Kerry Kennedy 📍 Brooklyn, New York | USA | April 20 | 3:00 pm

My windows don't open more than a couple of inches, but every night at 7 pm, I whoop and holler out of the narrow crack to join the city's appreciation cheers for medical staff and other essential workers.

It's tough being quarantined in a 600 square foot apartment; I live alone with four rescue cats (two are camera shy). I am happy to stay in, however, knowing I am doing my best not to further burden our hospitals or put vulnerable populations at more risk.

The only way to mentally and emotionally survive is to focus on the things we can control, remember all we have to be grateful for, and let go of the rest.

A beautiful side-effect of the pandemic: my building neighbors are connecting on Facebook, supporting each other's small businesses, doing grocery runs and lending supplies. Before this, not many of us ever spoke to each other. It's a strikingly ironic voluntary connection manifested through obligatory separation.

Mimi Robinton 📍 Tahoe Vista, California | USA | April 7 | 11:34 am

Joanne Marie Hoopes 📍 Rishikesh | India | April 26 | 9:00 am

India went into a lockdown quarantine on March 24. I've been living in India for over two years and I still get excited every time I see a monkey.

Theresa Alexander Gall 📍 Anaconda, Montana | USA | April 1 | 7:37 pm

Chuck Wysong 📍 Scotts Valley, California | USA | June 8 | 5:08 am

The star of the picture is Rudy, a Yorkshire Terrier. Cute little respite from the world.

Leanne Cummins 📍 Avondale, New South Wales | Australia | April 9 | 2:30 pm

Megan Buckley 📍 Hilldene, Victoria | Australia | April 4 | 5:18 pm

This is the view from our kitchen window, two of our pet camels came into the back yard for some green grass.

Diane Jhueck 📍 Langley, Washington | USA | April 21 | 7:25 am

I just buried my beloved dog, Holly, who was a few months short of 18 years old and died on Easter. She has many visitors to her grave each day, including bird seed stealing deer. The first thing I do in the morning now is look out this window and tell her how much I love her. Because of the pandemic, I was able to slow down and spend all those precious moments with her through her last breaths. I would love to know where you are in the world.

Nancy Gray 📍 Evergreen, Colorado | USA | April 16 | 7:21 pm

Kristin Freed 📍 Tehachapi, California | USA | April 16 | 10:00 am

Lucy Foster Neylan 📍 Bissel | Kenya | April 26 | 9:45 am

Geert van Kaathoven 📍 Plettenberg Bay | South Africa | April 23 | 4:10 pm

These nyalas come visit me almost every day!

Wendy Hamilton 📍 North Salt Lake, Utah | USA | March 7 | 9:51 am

Isa Peersman 📍 Hornsby Heights, New South Wales | Australia | April 5 | 5:31 pm

How lucky are we to live right on the bush of a national park. The birds are Cockatoos.

Howard Carbone 📍 Talkeetna, Alaska | USA | April 2 | 7:38 am

I'm hunkered down with my family. We've been entertained by three moose who've been hanging out for the past two weeks. They are ten times my size and have no fear of us and they can be dangerous if you get too close, but they are generally peaceful. They are here to escape deep snow in the woods and to eat the birch branches when we cut one down for firewood. Yesterday one came over and started eating a tree while I was still cutting it up. They are hungry enough to eat a Tony Crocetto painting!

Monica Lindqvist 📍 Uppsala | Sweden | April 5 | 11:00 am

I had a feeling that someone was watching me I turned around and saw this.

Claire Evans 📍 Catonsville, Maryland | USA | April 10 | 3:46 pm

Roofs of the world

A village dozes. A city sleeps. A town awakens.

Under the roofs that shelter us, we live our lives and fall in and out of love,
our joys and our misfortunes are concealed there.

Patchworks, patterns made up of interlacing curved lines.
The disordered intricacies of a great labyrinthine network.
Under a cloudy sky, the rain, the snow or the burning sun,
the roofs go on forever.

The rooftops reach out to one another and come together. You could go round the
world just by walking over them. Reach for the heights, engage with the sky and
flirt with the moon. Chat with the stars.

The roofs of the world are made up of a thousand different kinds of building
materials ranging from the finest to the most basic, from the long-lasting
to the temporary.

Traditional and industrial structures appear side by side in light-hearted chaos.
We may not live under the same roof, be it ceramic, slate, or clay, but we do
harbour the same feelings.

Under the roofs of the world, people sleep, dream, improve their minds,
converse with others and live in hope.

Micaela Pavoncello 📍 Rome | Italy | April 15 | 1:14 pm

Tonya Saner Sidoti 📍 Paris | France | April 15 | 1:33 pm

Joy Marie 📍 Baguio City | Philippines | April 29 | 3:03 pm

Sandesh Naidoo 📍 Kempton Park | South Africa | April 18 | 1:25 pm

Taly Johnson 📍 Manhattan, New York | USA | April 12 | 2:00 pm

We don't have a perfect vista of the New York skyline. We live in the back of a building, where we can regularly hear birds sing, and not traffic and loud city noise.

Nowadays, it's quiet anyway – in lockdown for many days – not counting. I still love the view, I can see a bit of Manhattan above roofs from my bedroom window, but I can also see the ivy that grows on the side of my building, the lights and shadows of unorganized cables, on the adjacent building, the one that blocks the perfect view. To me, this imperfection is wonderful! I can still see the tip of the Empire State Building, and feel very lucky to live in the most beautiful city in the world.

I Love New York more than ever!

Evgeny Slobodski 📍 Tel Aviv | Israel | April 18 | 7:08 pm

Natlina Sengmany Bangkok | Thailand | March 26 | 1:30 pm

Maria Parisi 📍 Venice | Italy | April 14 | 7:02 pm

Fan nette 📍 Quimper | France | April 3 | 9:00 am

Judit Tuna 📍 Budapest | Hungary | April 18 | 6:01 pm

Shefali Mitra 📍 Manali, Himachal Pradesh | India | April 10 | 7:00 pm

Behind the scene

A photo catches your attention.
You need the time to read, discover and enjoy a story.

Be it a slice of life or a family epic.
Each personal journey is like a picture book filled with memories, traumas, victories and defeats.
They tell a story somewhere between the shadows and the light.

This is a moment for disclosures, a time for sharing secrets.
Our stories can travel to faraway places.
A community of readers sits down to listen to them.
You grow fond of someone living on the other side of the world.

We feel compassion, tenderness and admiration for strangers
who are suddenly so close to us.

Let us share their joys, their grief, their anger, their highs and their lows.

KathGerard Lafferty 📍 Widgee, Queensland | Australia | April 27 | 7:00 am

ONE WORLD

As we sit with idle hands and an idle mind,

We scroll through Facebook to see what we can find.

Our eyes alight on views galore,

All corners of the world through someone's front door.

Views through your window, some resplendent in snow

Showing us places we currently can't go.

Sharing visions so different, yet of all the same

Timing is the now, and co-vid is the game.

We join as one as we travel afar

From the comfort of our chairs; no need for a car.

No money is spent on flights or fares

We rejoice in the beauty and share in the cares.

Thank you for sharing your home with us

Our connection is one, we unite with no fuss.

This time will pass and we'll move around once more

Let's retain the kindred spirit and leave open our front door.

Shantel Rich Chelmsford, Massachusetts | USA | April 10 | 11:27 am

My 83 year old mother lives in an attached in-law apartment on the back side of my home. This is a view of her back porch/patio from my living room window. On March 6th she decided it would be best to close the doors between our house and hers so she could be protected during the pandemic since she has several health challenges. It was a hard decision to make as we would normally see each other every day and eat dinner together every evening.

I realized on April 6th that it had been an entire month of her staying within her house and not going outside as it is still cold here this time of year. So I asked her to start doing "sunshine dates" with me on her back porch. She sits up on her porch in her chair and I sit on the patio far enough away to be safe, but close enough where I can actually see her and visit with her and we both get sunshine! We FaceTime every day, but it just isn't the same as seeing one another in person. I do feel blessed to be able to have her so close during this crazy time though, where I can take care of her and get her the things she needs so she doesn't have to go out.

Feel free to say hi to her - her name is Willa! Stay safe everyone, find the silver linings and love on your family!

Steven J. Whitfield Cairo | Egypt | April 28 | 6:00 pm

The sun sets on the pyramids as the call to prayer sounds and the streets begin to clear for iftar, the breaking of the fast for Ramadan.

In 2008 I attempted suicide. I was hospitalized and I lost everything. When I got out I lost my job, my car, my home, everything. I was 24 with no education outside of a high school diploma, and I knew only how to sell things to people, which I hated.

I dreamt of traveling the world and seeing new places but I'd done nothing close to that. I lost focus of everything. I thought money was the key to happiness and I chased that. Feeling devoid of everything, I really thought that there was no reason to continue. I had my shot at life and I blew it. My family convinced me to go back to university, despite my appeals that I was too old. I became a teacher, I volunteered as a coach for the Special Olympics, and I worked with at risk youth. I found that what made me happy was making kids who I could empathize with happy. Making them feel that they were cared for, that a stranger could invest in them, and believe in them. I haven't looked back since.

This situation has brought back old emotions, it's taken away from me so much of what I feel I need to be happy and I feel disconnected from the very humans I only want to better. I've had to adapt, and in that, I've come to see, slowly, that I have much to be grateful for.

Today I moved into my dream flat. I'm a kid from an extremely humble, and very young family in the desert of west Texas with a dream to travel the world and today I feel accomplished. My home today is a place I could only dream of as a child and couldn't fathom in 2008. I still struggle, every day in fact, but I know that I have a purpose, and through a laptop or in person, it doesn't matter, I know there are tiny humans who need to be believed in and I'm happy to do that! I loved every single student that I've had and I don't say that because it's what a teacher should say, I say it because I mean it. Today I feel OK, and that's always a step on the right direction for anyone.

Maria Scarvalone 📍 Brooklyn, New York | USA | April 17 | 6:08 pm

Here's the view from my front porch in Brooklyn, day 46 of our own self-imposed quarantine. My family is hardly leaving the house, doing our part to flatten the curve in our hard-hit city, which today has reached 12,287 dead (officially).

We normally spend a lot of time outside on our front porches, talking to our neighbors while kids play on the sidewalk and street. It's very quiet now, as we all try to social distance and spend most of the time indoors. But at 7 pm, we come out onto our front porches to cheer for all the healthcare workers working across the city to keep us safe. We wave to each other and reconnect in a moment of solidarity and gratitude for those risking their lives for us.

I love this group and what it shows of our beautiful world and common humanity.

Esther Kassovicz ⚲ Tel Aviv | Israel | April 11 | 5:49 pm

This is around 12:30 today 4.4.20 from my window in the Southern part of Tel Aviv, Israel... it's warm and dry weather around 26 Celsius degrees (about 79 Fahrenheit)...

The street is quiet but music is playing from many apartments: we just finished an online Zoom free dance session with about 60 participants, next door they're playing some very loud & happy oriental music and my neighbor is having her two young daughters jump and dance wildly, across in the other building someone is praying and singing some traditional Jewish songs with his family, from another entrance I can hear a classical cello musician practicing, while some foreign workers from Moldova are playing and dancing some Eastern European folk dances, while others are laughing and playing cards... on the whole, there's some more than usually lively Shabbat atmosphere...

One can better hear all the neighbors' activities since the traffic noise isn't interfering as usual. I find it interesting and quite surprising to feel the strong pulse of Life and even certain Peace in the hood. I'm grate to feel less intensity all around. Interesting times indeed... we're definitely into Staying Alive.

Beth Sightler Burlington, Vermont | USA | April 14 | 4:00 pm

I hurried to take a photo of this view from our kitchen just after I'd replaced 3 of the barn windows. For a short while all 58 panes are intact. As soon as my husband and sons return (they're grocery shopping for my mom) their quarantine energy will mean that arrows, footballs, rocks, frisbees, basketballs and other projectiles will start smashing out the panes again. And, honestly, that's ok with me. We've gotten wise and started replacing them with plexiglass - I keep a stack inside the first bay and I love that our boys are playing freely and wildly outside. This is a weird and temporary time home with family. We're reassessing what's important, working on our "Urban Farm", reverting to childhood games and devouring Netflix series at night. In the days we work hard. Inside the third bay a hen is sitting on a clutch of eggs - they should start hatching in the next 48 hours. Behind the garage are our gardens, goldfish pond, chickens, bee hives, big maple trees, fruit trees, baby greens and annuals are pushing into the spring. There's also a treehouse with all its windows knocked out.

And it's not all milk and honey. I'm the director of an organization that supports people with intellectual disabilities and autism and I spend my days making sure they and our staff are safe and supported. We provide residential, community, vocational and medical supports and the people in our system are at a high risk of bad outcomes if they contract the Covid-19 infection. We're concentrating on making sure people don't get sick and advocating for their lives to be as valued as anyone else's when they do. I am proud to be in Vermont where we're doing a good job flattening the curve, but we've had some hard losses.

Sending you love and wishes of good health in you're beautiful part of the world. I'm enchanted by the smaller, homey, modest views as much as the big, saucy, splashy ones. We're all here for a short time, finding beauty and people to love inside and outside the windows. Thanks for sharing mine.

Caroline O'Brien New Orleans, Louisiana | USA | April 8 | 8:50 am

We have oodles of fantastic architecture and beautiful streetscapes here in New Orleans. This photo may not depict that. But let me tell you about the woman who lives in that house, for she is a force to be reckoned with. I've lived here almost 11 years, the first 2 of which, Ms H didn't acknowledge me. There was never a lot of activity over there but every few weeks, ladies would pull up, wearing their church clothes (& I'm talking southern baptist African American church clothes - lots of all white outfits, lots of hats). Ms H would load foil covered trays into their cars and they would split. I used to wonder what her specialty was.

About 2 years after I moved in, I noticed a lot of activity over there. Folks I had never seen before congregating on her porch, propping each other up. It was obvious they were in mourning, not gathered to celebrate. I saw Ms H very early the next morning and told her I was scared to ask her what was going on at her place, that I was sure the news wasn't good. "They kilt my son." Was her reply. Her youngest son, riding his bike to visit a cousin at one of the then remaining housing projects in New Orleans, had been shot in broad daylight. Over 100 bullet casings were recovered at the scene. The worst part of this story is it turns out that her son wasn't even the guy the gang bangers were looking for - totally a case of mistaken identity.

Since then I've gotten beneath Ms H's gruff exterior. She talks to me now, when she feels like it. She has raised 3 children on her own, worked a custodial job at a local university for decades, kept current on the mortgage, and suffered through more health problems than any 60-some-thing year old in a first world country ought to endure. I've driven her to the emergency room more than once.

She barely tolerates the insanity that comes along with being a resident of this crazy city. I asked her one year if she planned to watch the Mardi Gras parade that day and she replied "I don't fool with alla that, me." (I love when I meet someone here who has that strange colloqui-alism of tacking me on to the end of every sentence.)

Ms H was treated for cancer in January. I have only seen her once since St Patrick's Day when she was coming back from the grocery. Despite the fact that every neighbor on the block has told her we'll go get her whatever she needs. Her oldest, who is some form of traveling medical professional (CNA maybe, I'm not sure) has been here since the stay at home order went into effect. But i guess he's been no more successful than the rest of have been in convincing her to let us do for her.

Think good thoughts for Ms H's continued good health. And maybe say a prayer that she'll break down and let someone take care of her for a change.

Pearl Galbraith 📍 Whitefish, Montana | USA | April 23 | 7:24 pm

After seeing such spectacular views from tropical and warm places on this site, I questioned how I would capture my view for the past 20 years of pine trees, overgrown vegetation and a tired dirt road. I walked around to several windows and just sighed at how plain and boring it all looked. Then I opened the front door and was captured by the beauty of what I saw.

An evening rain had just passed and rays of sun were coming through the clouds and lighting up the trees. My eyes focused on my husband's grandfather's rocking chair and it was like I was seeing it for the very first time. The chair was given to us years ago and with no place to put it I had simply left it on the porch. Now placed beside the old milk cans holding dollar store flowers, the chair seems to be sending a message from days gone by. A message from quieter times when lingering on porches was a norm, not a luxury. Personally I have never even sat in the chair, but simply through the activity of taking this picture, I know that will change. This season of Covid, of forced slow down, of reduced activity, of global common ground, is showing up in our lives as a gift. Up until now life for my family was too busy to be porchin. Yet today, that changes. I am going to sit a spell in grandpa's chair and breathe deeply.

Life is precious. Take time to smell the flowers. Be safe.

Where in the world are you taking time to sit a spell?

Lonneke Bank 📍 Guangzhou | China | April 7 | 4:07 pm

This is the view from my window in Guangzhou, China, this afternoon at about 4 pm. We live in Guangzhou since 2016 for my husband's work.

The coronavirus started to influence the life of my family half January. We were in Sri Lanka for our Chinese New Year holiday when the panic in China started. As my husband's company had forbidden us to go back to China we decided to fly to our home country, the Netherlands. With three suitcases full of summer clothes. In the meanwhile we heard from friends in China that life had completely stopped there due to all the heavy measurements taken by the Chinese government to block the virus.

In the beginning of March the situation in China seemed to be safe enough for my husband to go back and start working again. I decided to stay a little longer in the Netherlands as our kids (8 and 6) could go to school there, whereas schools in China were still closed. Only two days after my husband had left we spoke on the phone and concluded that we should have gone with him to Guangzhou as the virus was growing fast in Europe. We were afraid that the virus might split us up as a family. The first flight back to China that we could get was on the 13th of March. Until that date we kept our fingers crossed that it wouldn't get cancelled, as many did, but we were lucky: on Saturday the 14th I landed with my sons early in the morning at Guangzhou airport. The rest of the day we were held by the Chinese authorities dressed in welcoming white suits, having to fill in forms and answer questions about our health and travel history and to do several temperature checks. Without any explanation about the procedure and how long they would keep us – quite frightening. After 12 hours we were finally brought home (with an ambulance with the sirens on – ?!?) and reunited with my husband. Then 14 days of home quarantine and two corona tests for the whole family followed.

Now, almost two weeks later, we feel relatively safe and free. Life in China is slowly getting back to normal (except for the schools still being closed in our province), although most people are still very afraid to go out of their houses. And a 'second wave' of the virus is also feared much here. Personally my biggest fear now is that something bad will happen to someone dear to us in Europe. As China has closed its borders and many countries in Europe as well, we might not be able to make it back home.

Our life has been quite a roller coaster in the last few months. However, I realize very well how blessed we are. To have been able to take a plane to a safe place twice now - not everyone has this opportunity. And to be together as a family, all of us healthy.

Take care everyone out there facing the virus!

Irene Forcella Rome | Italy | April 25 | 2:50 pm

Today, 25th April 2020, we celebrate Italy's uprising against Nazi-Fascist rule. At 3 pm local time, we stood at our windows and on our balconies and sang *Bella Ciao*, our resistance song. This year, we celebrate our own private and collective resistance. In some parts of Italy, Covid-19 has almost swept away a generation, those who fought for our freedom, which we are now asked to temporarily forfeit in order to protect us all and the elderly in particular.

This is a view from my small flat in Rome, Italy, which is pleasantly located just outside a park, currently under lockdown too. Here, the big city becomes a small village, where you hang your washing next to your neighbour's and isolation is easier to bear.

The lockdown has hit many in our community, especially the most vulnerable. Some of us in our neighbourhood – like in many other parts of the country – are liaising with civil protection agencies and distributing food and personal hygiene products to those who cannot provide for their families and who are not reached by public aid. Some of them have never had to ask before but we know that we can only get through this as a community.

In this picture: a quarantine Italian flag.

I love to see all your views. Stay safe and strong.

Nou Mija Staten Island, New York | USA | April 21 | 2:00 pm

I am a nurse in NYC taking care of positive Corona post partum patients.

I am cordoned off from rest of my family: 93 year old Mom. 90 year old father. 14 year old daughter & immunocompromised brother with cancer.. A wall of plastic sheet separates my bed & bath from rest of home. My family leaves plates of food for me to pick up on the back porch.

This is my view from back door of porch. I wave to my family through the door & window of the back porch. Everyone is helping... Team Spirit... In this together...

Shelley Finch ● Sea Point, Cape Town | South Africa | April 25 | 9:58 am

We are entering our 5th week of lockdown and ours has been one of the most strictest in the world - no going outdoors unless for essential grocery shopping, no exercising outside, no dog walking.

In the distance is the ocean that I used to walk along every morning with a hot coffee in my hand. I would see all the people living in these flats walking their dogs, pushing their children in prams, enjoying a picnic on the grass. Not for a moment did I even think I would miss people I don't know so much.

Every night at 8 pm the neighbourhood erupts with the sound of clapping and cheering for our essential workers. The sound bounces off the walls of the tall buildings and echos across the street. For some people who live alone like me, it's the only sound they hear each day that reminds them that there is still a world full of people out there.

Pamela Grant 📍 Victoria, British Columbia | Canada | April 16 | 1:05 pm

This is my friend's garden. Her name was Justine and she died on March 3 of cancer, exactly three weeks before her 56th birthday. I am staying here, slowly packing the last of her things up and looking after her cats, who will soon be leaving this island for another, where they will live with her daughter. This was where we would drink coffee, wine, read books and nap in the sun. I will miss this view, almost as much as I miss her.

Stacy Lowe 📍 New York City, New York | USA | April 8 | 4:30 pm

I am a surgical nurse from Louisville, Kentucky here to help fight Covid-19 and to give my fellow nurses reprieve. This is the view from the Marriott Marquis on Broadway from my hotel window. I've made many sacrifices to be here because this is where I was led. NYC will now always have a place in my heart! Together we've got this! Pic taken 4-8-20. I'm here till 5-12-20.

Feast your eyes

Spectacular views of magnificent valleys, unsurpassed panoramas, idyllic landscapes. Sensational views follow one another.

Call it Heaven on earth or the garden of Eden; the scene is breathtaking.

The fauna and flora are all dressed up in their party finery.
Heaven and earth have come together, and the result is amazing.

Not to be outdone, the architecture allows for every creative whim.
Extravagant buildings and daring innovations that make your head spin.
Human creative ingenuity has been at work here.

Beauty has reached its apex.

Everywhere, from the very heart of the cities to the depths of the forests.
From the estuaries of the great rivers, and to the foot of the snow-capped mountains, beauty confidently reveals its charms. Who would argue with that?

Coreena Fletcher Draper, Utah | USA | April 14 | 7:45 pm

Jacqueline Garellick Senja island | Norway | April 2 | 2:25 am

Breathtaking views of the northern lights dancing outside our living room on day 17 of quarantine.
We live in a beautiful world and we have to take care of it.

Manisha Shah Bel Air, Mahe | Seychelles | March 24 | 4:15 pm

Misty Dawn Rigdon Colorado Springs, Colorado | USA | April 28 | 8:08 pm

Eastern slope of the Rocky Mountains with America's Mountain, Pike's Peak, in the center. To the south is NORAD and the new Space Force and to the north, the United States Air Force Academy.

A morning sunrise picture would also show the Garden of the Gods in the foreground. We are staying 'safer at home' by working remotely, learning remotely, teaching remotely and making masks for those who have to work with the public.

This deck and the patio below it have been the site of many Zoom/Skype sessions with business partners, students, friends, and family. One of our favorite activities with the family has been playing video trivia as a team with aunt Lori in Hannibal, MO; daughter Kelsey in Greenville, SC; and sister, Jessica in Peyton, CO.

Viktor Kessler Bishkek | Kyrgyzstan | April 12 | 7:00 am

Kate Barker ⬦ Dubai | United Arab Emirates | April 17 | 11:00 pm

I'm an Australian moved from Singapore to Dubai on my own, 2 days before a very strict 2-month lockdown and am yet to build my circle of friends here. I am fortunate to be able to work from home. I've not always had such a spectacular view, and have worked hard to get here. So no matter where you are THANK YOU, everyone for your posts. The sense of community is real. #weareinthistogether

Margarita Zobnina Moscow | Russia | April 14 | 7:30 pm

Holly Shepherd Lugano | Switzerland | April 11 | 10:57 am

Oana Bogdan ⦿ Brussels | Belgium | April 26 | 8:35 pm

My view is the European Parliament. As an architect, I wonder what will happen to the buildings of all these European institutions around me. Now that the jump to the digital world has been made, it seems improbable that the EU will consume so many resources to keep a huge physical presence here. Will the (too) many office buildings in my neighbourhood transform into housing?

Kimmernaq Kjeldsen Nuuk | Greenland | April 9 | 8:37 pm

Jo Handley Dubai | United Arab Emirates | April 6 | 6:32 pm

Shushanik Nersesyan Yerevan | Armenia | April 8 | 6:09 pm

Stacey Booth Fort Steele, British Colombia | Canada | April 28 | 11:01 am

Taken this morning as some deer casually graze in our front yard.

Ryan Terpstra Forest Grove, Oregon | USA | April 12 | 6:30 pm

Minna Rajalin-Käkönen Tammela | Finland | April 23 | 7:00 pm

Kathryn Taylor ♀ Wylie, Texas | USA | April 26 | 10:20 am

Tara Bisogna ⚲ Arco | Italy | April 26 | 8:38 pm

Balazs Cserne Dubai | United Arab Emirates | April 6 | 6:43 pm

We are grateful for nature's reward during the sunsets, if there are a few clouds present. Despite the lockdown we are enjoying our time with my wife as we are expecting our first baby, so it is magical to experience these days together. The only way out of this is to stay grateful for the little miracles in life! Keep positivity, share the love, count your blessings and help one another selflessly! Stay safe and healthy wherever you are in the world! Wishing you all the best!

Marianne Sunde Hestetun Kvitsøy | Norway | April 6 | 10:50 am

Sky Muhammad ⦿ Bishkek | Kyrgyzstan | April 17 | 9:00 am

Mid-morning sun over the slopes of the Ala-Archa National Park in the Tien Shan Mountains.

Håkan Wirtén Jönköping | Sweden | March 20 | 6:17 pm

Kristín Eva Einarsdóttir Þjórsárdalur | Iceland | April 18 | 8:16 am

Glenn Kincaid Castle Valley, Utah | USA | April 6 | 7:37 pm

Esmeraldo Chiodini Neto Guaramirim | Brazil | April 5 | 2:00 pm

Eva Trubetskaya Miami Beach, Florida | USA | April 12 | 8:00 pm

Linda Westbrook Pitt Town, New South Wales | Australia | April 25 | 6:45 am

Anzac Day - Lest We Forget

It was 100 years ago when Australians returned from the First World War, and on their first Anzac Day in Australia, it was in the middle of the Spanish flu. And so something very similar to what we will face today as we gather together without the parades, but we do so quietly and commemoratively.

This year we stand in our driveways at 6.00 am with candles to Light Up The Dawn. We remember those who fought for us, thank them for their service, let them know they're all appreciated, much admired and greatly respected.

This Anzac Day will be one to remember for a very long time.

Bára Hallgrímsdóttir Borgarnes | Iceland | April 27 | 10:30 pm

Susan Rabe Bloubergstrand, Cape Town | South Africa | April 24 | 6:02 pm

Graham Ford Hong Kong | China | April 11 | 10:19 am

View south towards the Tsing Ma Bridge with Hong Kong Island beyond.

Lillian Scoles Whakatane | New Zealand | April 9 | 3:08 pm

Debbie Rodriguez Rio Rancho, New Mexico | USA | April 17 | 1:00 pm

Ajoy Edwards ♀ Darjeeling | India | March 30 | 7:13 am

Bjørg Elin Håkegård Jakobsen Svolvær | Norway | April 1 | 7:45 am

Rachel Kallenberg Ireland Tuckasegee, North Carolina | USA | April 19 | 6:47 am

Kjell-Erik Ruud Utne | Norway | March 27 | 6:00 pm

Daily life

It makes no demands.
It is our daily life.

The sun comes up, and the sun goes down,
one day follows the next.

In a place full of simple joys,
details make all the difference.
There is a delicate enchantment in tiny things.

Far away from the spheres of glamour, sophistication and exquisite surroundings.
We are here in our neighbourhoods, with our families and friends close by.

And above our heads, the sky is clear or changeable, mild or threatening.
In the same way as our lives are all similar, yet all different.

This is our world.

Sabrina Fall 📍 Kaolack | Senegal | April 9 | 12:00 pm

Temperature is average 40 °C. It will be 47 °C in 2 hours.

I just came back to bring some water to sheep and goats which live on the rooftop. They belong to my husband's sister. We live there with my husband's mother, my husband's sister, nephews and my baby (and my dog!). We planted bougainvilliers (pink flowers) 2 years ago when I quit France to live in Sénégal.

Nghi Tram 📍 Brussels | Belgium | March 24 | 5:38 pm

Unfortunately we live in a small apartment in Brussels and don't have a garden... but we do have a quite decent sized terrace (without sun).

Our view is not the greatest but our sky is blue and we have a dog so we enjoy nice walks around the neighbourhood.

Arianna Mereu 📍 Florence | Italy | April 12 | 5:20 pm

We hardly ever enjoyed our balcony before: it was home for our cactus and not much more. Since we are in quarantine (over a month, now) this tiny terrace has become: a swimming pool for toys, a solarium, a restaurant, a stage for neighborhood concerts, a library, a cafeteria, a launch pad for soap bubbles.

Even if we don't have a garden or any outdoor space, we feel blessed. Stay safe and enjoy what you have!

Maristela Salvatori 📍 Porto Alegre | Brazil | April 2 | 8:42 am

Chiara S. Arcadipane ♀ Genova | Italy | April 23 | 1:52 pm

Not really a view because I live in the medieval old Town of Genova in Italy.

Things are strange, surreal I must say, frightening too I must admit. As I said I live in the medieval city centre of Genova, the building where my flat is dates back from 1400.

I am alone at home, looking towards the little bit of sun I'm entitled to at this time of the year and thinking that what we're facing seems too big for us. Indeed it's not, we're fighting. Playing music from our homes all together, clapping our hands. There's a sense of community that you do not exactly feel in this country in everyday normal life.

We must look all together at that ray of light through the buildings. We've got to reach that light all together and we will. We all will, everywhere on this planet.

Love to you all.

Melissa Wistehuff ⦿ Raleigh, North Carolina | USA | April 28 | 6:00 pm

This is my view from our porch in Raleigh, North Carolina, on April 28 at 6:00 pm. If you look closely, you can see our pet guinea fowl and goats ready for their supper. My family – my husband, three children, lots of animals, and I – are on week 7 of quarantine and week three of online schooling. We feel very fortunate to have a yard that is fun and full of life with critters, gardens, toys and activities.

This time is giving me a chance to reflect on what is most important, and what I want to welcome back into our lives when this is all over. This page has been such a respite for me, and thanks to all of your lovely pictures, I keep adding places that I want to visit when we are able. What an amazingly beautiful world in which we live!

Please tell us where you are, as I have a world map that I'm going to have the kids mark for each location that is named. Sending a virtual high five to all our fellow self-isolators!

Gianna Giorgio 📍 Phoenix, Arizona | USA | April 24 | 6:20 am

This afternoon I and my 10-year-old granddaughter and 13-year-old grandson (they and their parents live here) will be participating in a birthday parade for an 11-year-old boy who lives a few blocks north of us. (For the last few weeks, neighborhood social media has been listing children in the area who can't have an-person birthday party and scheduling the parades; at the appointed time, people drive by the home in their cars decorated with balloons, wave, honk their horns, display big homemade cards, etc.).

We don't know the birthday boy, but his dad wrote that he had asked if they were going to die from this virus, not what an 11 year old should be worrying about on his birthday. So, we'll make a big poster card and decorate the car, and we'll join the parade, and honk and yell, and shoot bubbles with the new bubble gun. And we will all celebrate and be joyous and help this boy have a happy birthday.

Bonga Zamisa 📍 Cape Town | South Africa | April 29 | 11:50 am

Stéphanie Taillandier 📍 Palermo | Italy | March 29 | 5:07 pm

Adela Driver 📍 Grande Prairie, Alberta | Canada | March 29 | 10:50 am

Lars-Anders Gronewold 📍 Cork | Ireland | April 18 | 9:40 am

This is part of an old Convent. Behind the bushes you would see the old cemetery for the nuns.

Shirel Kadambari Horovitz 📍 Tel Aviv | Israel | April 20 | 12:55 pm

This is the view from my apartment in south Tel Aviv, Israel at noon today. I consider myself really lucky to have a roof over my head and even a piece of sky to look at. And yes, I can actually see into the living room across from me + watch his tv when it's on. Neighbors business is everybody's business in this hood.

Bernd Rathjen 📍 Berlin | Germany | April 26 | 7:00 pm

Jenny Clark 📍 Yulara, Northern Territory | Australia | April 18 | 4:09 pm

My view is typical of the Central Australian Desert. I live in staff housing in the Resort Village of Yulara Northern Territory. Usually at this time of year the 4 hotels & campground are bustling with tourists who have travelled from all over the world to the middle of Australia to visit the UNESCO World Heritage listed Uluru-Kata Tjuta National Park.

Due to Covid-19 all accomodation is closed and hundreds of staff have been stood down & have left town. Our airport has closed and the closest town Alice Springs is a 4.5 hour drive, with any trip there requiring a 2 week quarantine before you're able to return home. There have been no cases of Covid here and the authorities are doing their best to ensure it remains this way.

I'm not exactly sure how many of us are still in town as everyone is self isolating. Some like my husband are still working; carrying out essential duties & maintenance.

Thanks to all who are sharing their special place.... stay safe & stay home.

Michael Rhys 📍 Tokyo | Japan | April 12 | 9:59 am

A view from our porch that looks out over the temple next door and its small graveyard.

Robin Harrison 📍 Gig Harbor, Washington | USA | April 27 | 7:28 pm

Eugin Robinson 📍 Bangalore | India | April 1 | 5:30 pm

Bangalore, India. This is the part of my neighbourhood I have been seeing through the window of my new workplace (one of the bedrooms in my apartment, that is) for the last two weeks.

It is always unchanging, except now for someone (if you look earnestly enough into the picture) looking into a window from the balcony of one of those distant housing blocks across an arid stretch of land. I see two cars eternally parked there in the small road. An old Tata Sierra and a Maruti Suzuki Celerio. I see the same calves browsing whatever shrubbery left in the vacant plot, day in and day out with their mother cow reclining somewhere in the vicinity, lost in some bovine reverie. Sometimes a flock of mynas, to the greatest joy of my heart, swoop down and peck at the ground for food and with the same joyful frenzy they soar and fly away in unison, leaving my heart yearn for their return.

These sights are not in anyway remarkable. They are nondescript, forlorn. But they are imbued with some sort of poignancy which they did not hitherto have. I look out through the window, taking a brief break from work, and at these mundane dealings of reality, almost frozen in time, lean back and sigh deeply, as if some impending calamity is upon the world, or, if I am sipping a cup of tea, there would arise a glimmer of hope and a swarm of infinite possibilities in the horizon of my deeply vexed being.

Sirkku Hölttä 📍 Las Palmas de Gran Canaria | Spain | April 14 | 2:00 pm

Rachel Qnc 📍 Kiev | Ukraine | March 22 | 12:14 pm

Nadezda Nezvanova 📍 Bologna | Italy | April 12 | 4:15 pm

Kate Bringardner 📍 San Miniato, Pisa | Italy | April 3 | 8:51 am

This is the view from my kitchen window. Not the most glamorous but I take great comfort that daily rituals, like laundry, are still happening. The simplest of routines provides hope and a touch of normal in an abnormal time.

Mandy Halse 📍 Krakow | Poland | April 19 | 12:47 pm

The glorious view from the balcony of our apartment! No workmen today as it's Sunday, but they'll be starting up again at 7 am tomorrow morning.

We moved into this Airbnb apartment when Poland closed its borders on the 16th March. I'd read less than positive reviews about the construction work, but it's been wonderful to hear the workmen going on with life as normal and to see the trains go by... our link to the outside world while we're inside in self-imposed isolation.

We didn't actually have a home to go to as have been travelling long-term, so consider ourselves incredibly fortunate to have been in Krakow when borders started closing, as the supermarkets have been well-stocked, there are pallets of toilet paper and pasta in the aisles, and the Polish people have handled this pandemic with a calm certainty... we love it here and are happy to stay as long as the state of epidemic is in place.

Lauren Cunningham 📍 Lower Chittering, Western Australia | Australia | April 16 | 9:52 am

So lucky the kids have this space during iso to continue running around.

Trampoline to burn off energy and that sand is where we are building them a BMX track. The logs are a bit of a nature playground. And the strip of green is a golf green where they hit balls to the small hole down in the bottom corner.

There's currently a movement out here called "camping at home" for Easter, so the kids set up the tent and have been sleeping in there since we could go away this year.

Yes it's brown in our summer, but in winter everything's green and lush. Wouldn't want to do iso anywhere else.

Timothy Sinaguglia 📍 Woodside, New York | USA | April 20 | 10:00 am

I live in Queens, about five blocks from Jackson Heights. This has been one of the areas hardest hit by the pandemic. I suppose it's only fitting that I'm just getting over a mean two week case of stay-at-home Covid! The view from my room of the backyard isn't much to look at, and I usually just keep the blinds down because of the lack of privacy. The coils of electric wires don't offer much in the way of aesthetic pleasures!

It's an efficiency dwelling for a recently out of work barista and artist in New York City.

Cons aside, this is a quiet, warm and well insulated room. It gets a good amount of light, and I can barely hear traffic or street noise. Even birdsong puts in an appearance at odd moments. I'm just grateful to be recovering and that I didn't need hospitalization.

Peace and love, folks!

Lea Schmeling 📍 Berlin | Germany | April 28 | 11:33 am

No garden, no balcony, no spectacular view and because of the current situation also no job anymore...

But we are healthy and that is what counts...

We are using these difficult times for being creative... This "Kiez" (Berlin does not really have a city centre but many districts - Kieze - with their own centres) has always been famous for its creativity. Just around the corner is the house that David Bowie lived in when he shared an apartment with Iggy Pop in the 70s...

So we are busy learning instruments, painting, renovating, homeschooling and dreaming of visiting some of your homes once everything is over...

The almost ten year old is just a little sad that there will probably not be a birthday party this year (1st of June). Shout out, if you want to send him a postcard as a birthday greeting, he would love that!

United colours

Never-ending shades of colour on life's palette,
nature is an artist, and we are its joyful assistants.

We dream in colours: blue for lagoons, red for our passions and green for our hopes.
Our feelings too are like colours. Our expectations are every colour of the rainbow.
Whether they exist in association, in harmony or in contrast,
different shades merge together and oppose one another,
turning everything into pure magic.

Our walls, our terraces, our houses and our gardens are superb illustrations
of this phenomenon.

Expertly mixed hues, monochrome surfaces.
Colour is the source of pleasure.
Colour is of the essence.

Colour is freedom.

Gary Wornell 📍 Kathmandu | Nepal | April 27 | 10:00 am

View from my terrace looking toward the foothills of the Himalayas - as close to heaven as you can get.

Shannon Hartman Cannings 📍 Lubbock, Texas | USA | April 11 | 2:25 pm

I painted my new fence to look like 170 different colored pencils. It has been my pandemic therapy.

Kim Klein 📍 Erie, Colorado | USA | April 23 | 9:20 am

When you can't find a rainbow, make one yourself.

Inco Saito 📍 Tokyo | Japan | April 29 | 9:30 am

This says 'KOINOBORI' and is a traditional decoration to raise in Children's Day of May so that a child is brought up in good health.

Luca Pacchioni 📍 Geneva | Switzerland | April 5 | 5:48 pm

Kim Auld Miner 📍 Howard, Colorado | USA | April 15 | 6:24 am

Babette Coppin 📍 Setúbal | Portugal | April 5 | 4:00 pm

Janice Dowdeswell 📍 Whanganui | New Zealand | April 14 | 10:21 am

Dorothy Arriola Colby 📍 Punaluu, Hawaii | USA | April 11 | 8:35 am

Origami garland made by my daughter in celebration of her brother's wedding that happened on Leap Day, right before the lockdowns started.

Colleen Kissinger 📍 Ajijic | Mexico | March 26 | 6:14 pm

Sierra Madres in the background. The lovely Jacarandas in bloom...

Susan Speed Charleston, South Carolina | USA | April 14 | 7:10 pm

Jonna Poulsen 📍 Narsaq | Greenland | April 12 | 10:00 am

Due to Covid 19 our capital city Nuuk is closed for rest of the world, including for me who should have traveled to Nuuk 11-04-2020.

Ingrid van den Boogaard 📍 Villajoyosa | Spain | April 6 | 2:29 pm

Windows from my window

Open one window and discover other windows.
They offer glimpses into people's lives and their stories.
These stories are unique.

We follow daily events by looking through one window into another.
They harbour our passions, our loves, our problems. And also our dreams.
People follow their own paths. Everyone is different.

We call one another, we congratulate one another, we catch up on family news.
We invite each other to cocktail and dinner parties while maintaining our distances.

We chat in the shade of our balconies.

A child's laughter, a grandfather's hoarse voice. A snatch of jazz music
from the radio, a dog barking, the creaking of a shutter closing.
Sounds criss-cross, mingle, accumulate and multiply.
Like a little piece of atmospheric music.

Comforting noises.

Gabriella Porcu 📍 Barcelona | Spain | April 17 | 1:34 pm

Lou Lou 📍 Paris | France | April 26 | 8:00 pm

Bety Dimant 📍 Rio de Janeiro | Brazil | April 15 | 5:40 pm

View from my window, I see nature explaining itself and the silence...

Jennifer Zsürger 📍 São Paulo | Brazil | April 12 | 12:00 pm

Solitude.

Patrick Le Dez 📍 Rennes | France | April 5 | 9:15 pm

Griffen Herrera 📍 San Francisco, California | USA | April 24 | 11:58 am

Hisham Youssef 📍 Shanghai | China | April 26 | 1:00 pm

This is such a basic view that shows the monotony of residential neighborhoods of many areas in Shanghai. My other view is a distant one of the Shanghai Tower. I am staying safe but then again, we are not in lockdown as much of the world is these days.

Patrícia Azevedo Névoa 📍 Almada | Portugal | April 14 | 8:15 am

Manuela Porcu 📍 Savona | Italy | April 11 | 2:00 pm

This is the view from a window on shared courtyard on day 32 of lockdown. On the other side I can see the Ligurian Sea but it's unreachable. So I prefer this view, at least I can hope to have a few words with some neighbour.

Michela Fabbri 📍 Faenza, Emilia Romagna | Italy | April 12 | 8:45 am

I wake up, open my window, take a deep breath, smile and feel gratitude for another lovely, sunny day. Just waiting for my neighbours to come outside their balconies and start our daily funny chats. A great opportunity to finally know each other better. Happy Easter and take care!

Gisela Milman 📍 Rio de Janeiro | Brazil | April 3 | 2:28 pm

This is the view from my window. Despite living in Rio de Janeiro, a city with some of the most beautiful natural scenery, from every window in my home I see windows, very close, and I see my neighbors in their homes. I see families having dinner together, I see children dancing in front of the TV, I see people reading books, couples cooking together, I see father and son training judo, kids playing soccer in their tiny balconies, I see elderly people exercising or trying to catch the little sun that comes through the windows. I see everyone at home.

Nikolas Giakoumidis 📍 Thessaloniki | Greece | April 26 | 4:18 pm

Marie-Catherine Mars 📍 Nice | France | March 24 | 1:23 pm

Enrico Rodriguez Barone 📍 Naples | Italy | March 15 | 11:13 am

Dolli Melaine 📍 Belgrade | Serbia | April 11 | 3:41 pm

I like the mystery of this view... My last room had an amazing view... But this one strikes my imagination... Peaceful days everyone!

Irene LaVon Walker 📍 Detroit, Michigan | USA | April 29 | 8:51 am

Day 46 of staying at home. For the first time since this began I am leaving the safety of our house today to go sew hospital gowns for those on the front lines. While not the kind of work I was doing before all this began, I'm glad my skills will be able to help others.

Isabelle Cyr ● Paris | France | April 11 | 7:33 pm

My courtyard in Paris. Every evening our neighbours and I come together at our windows, clapping for the medics who are saving lives while we stay cosy home. It feels like a small community.

Julie Thaler 📍 New York City, New York | USA | April 13 | 1:00 pm

Barkaszi Dóra 📍 Budapest | Hungary | April 28 | 2:00 pm

This is not the most beautiful picture in this group for sure, but I have flowers.

We live next to the Castle (I think the most beautiful area in Budapest) but still, if I look outside, I can see the inner courtyard, that is very typical of the houses of old Budapest. We have many windows but all of them faces the inner courtyards of this house (there are 3 of them strangely).

I did not plan this quarantine when we just moved here last summer. The Danube is 50 m away and the Castle is almost empty now since the tourists are home so we can still go outside safely for walks. It is strange that this district is a little treasurebox and feels like as if we were living in a village though we are just in the middle of the capital city. I cannot get enough of historical buildings around me and we have slower life here -at least I feel this.

Next time I will buy a house or flat with a garden for sure even if I consider the whole Castle to be my garden. Stay safe everyone.

Yosara Geerlings 📍 Amsterdam | The Netherlands | March 26 | 8:54 pm

Out of the picture

This is an unusual and rare scene.
It takes very little for ordinary things to become extraordinary.

It is a vision that challenges our opinions, plays havoc with our senses
and feeds our imagination.
Elated, it runs about here, there and everywhere.

We watch or act in an enjoyable play, combining thrills, laughter and emotion.
It's all about encounters.

Random, surprising and unexpected encounters.

That is the spice of life,
like the kick of champagne,
giving your body and your mind a high.

Kamo Toshiko 📍 Kakegawa-City, Shizuoka | Japan | April 29 | 7:04 am

Actually, the 90th birthday morning of my father. He made this beautiful green house.

Helen Huitink 📍 Orange City, Iowa | USA | April 13 | 1:30 pm

Léo Favreau 📍 Boursay | France | April 16 | 2:30 pm

We live in an old railway station. No train goes through there any longer but the railway tracks are still there. So from my window, I can dream of going away on a trip.

Eyal Izhar 📍 Tel Aviv | Israel | March 8 | 12:37 pm

Sport outside is limited, the roof is the gym.

Michele Arsenault 📍 New York City, New York | USA | April 22 | 5:06 pm

This was taken yesterday from my apartment building rooftop where I try to walk and breathe at least once a day. Perfect spot for weather system watching too. On this day, we were under a tornado watch (seems to be happening with greater frequency last few years), gale force winds, bursts of bright sunlights, scattered thunderstorms and a severe drop in temperature (last night plummeted to 35 degrees). Yes, we New Yorkers "have it all." Not bragging, just sayin'.

Mike Boivin 📍 Hollywood, California | USA | April 2 | 9:26 am

CNN Los Angeles building and the Hollywood sign as seen from my roof deck.

Jules Griffith 📍 Tromsø | Norway | March 31 | 11:26 am

Normally we have a view of the fjord. This year, not so much.

Jeannette Gory 📍 Abu Dhabi | United Arab Emirates | April 13 | 7:00 pm

A small town in the sand, these buildings are all company accommodations, housing workers for the oil refinery, nuclear power plant, etc. The apartments on the other side of the building face the desert. Sky clouded over, overnight was the first rain we've had in about a month.

Iwamoto Okazaki Marie 📍 Tokyo | Japan | March 25 | 9:27 am

Hope to see all of you from all over the world next year after we get over this crisis.

Asya Sergeeva 📍 Esch-sur-Alzette | Luxembourg | April 17 | 10:05 am

Janine Arlidge 📍 Maui, Hawaii | USA | April 28 | 8:56 am

I could have posted the lush greenery palm trees etc. But this is the most moving to me.

A young boy living alone with his mom. We daily put up animals or paintings. I thought I was doing this for him. But today realized it's for me as well. I love my view.

Tiffany Jump 📍 Puerto Penasco | Mexico | April 26 | 1:52 pm

I decided to do a little "yard work" today while quarantined.

Teri Dempski 📍 Loveland, Colorado | USA | April 16 | 3:10 pm

Donna Bryant 📍 Peoria, Arizona | USA | April 19 | 5:27 pm

Camila Ceretta 📍 Garruchos, Rio Grande do Sul | Brazil | April 16 | 7:37 am

Patricia Gilligan 📍 Bainbridge Island, Washington | USA | April 26 | 5:23 pm

El Smith 📍 New Orleans, Louisiana | USA | April 20 | 7:00 pm

Janet McPherson 📍 Reno, Nevada | USA | April 26 | 7:00 am

This just floated by our house – took this pic from my bedroom slider – what a nice way to start the day in isolation!

Kate Wilson 📍 Moab, Utah | USA | April 9 | 7:34 pm

We embarked on a grand adventure to travel the states starting March 2020. Two weeks in each spot. Been 'stuck' here ever since. The dirt bikes, college kids and four wheelers have all gone, replaced by wild cottontail bunnies, meandering cows and incredibly serene sunsets.

Enjoy the peace from your window, all of your photos are just stunning.

Pandora Jane 📍 Barcelona | Spain | April 23 | 2:00 pm

It may be a view of a wall but it's the best wall to look at! Looking left and right we can see two beautiful plazas as well. The wall is said to date back to the 1770s. It is Catalan style sgraffito decorative technique.

Jill Mohry 📍 Schwenksville, Pennsylvania | USA | April 14 | 10:25 am

USA is still inconsistent with it's stay-at-home/lockdown/quarantine orders depending on where you live. My town has been in quarantine for over a month.

I am a first grade teacher, so all of those post-its are schedules, reminders, notes... it's been quite an adjustment to say the least. But seeing their sweet faces on Zoom, watching them check out their toothless smiles, and hearing their awesome stories is the sunshine in my day.

I do love this tree though. There are at least 4 different bird species that share it. Every time I start worrying about students, my family, the world... I look out my window, hear birds singing their lovely songs, and it reminds me to just breathe.

I wish health, basic necessities, sanity, and peace to all of you. And hope- always hope.

Tia Gavin 📍 New York City, New York | USA | April 21 | 6:45 pm

New York, New York. We moved here partially to escape the Northern California fires - now this.

We're in a very nice but VERY small apartment on the upper east side. One living room window is large and from it you can see a tree and a bit of sky. But our other windows look out on buildings.

We walk early weekday mornings in Central Park, and then put our masks on the radiator to dry when we return. This was taken moments before the 7:00 cheers for our healthcare workers. We are one block from Lenox Hill Hospital and the cheers are louder each day. We are so grateful to have shelter and food, and for all of those putting their lives on the line. It's lovely to hear from people all over the world in this group, and to see your breathtaking (and humble) views.

Peace to you all.

Sébastien Decamps 📍 San Francisco, California | USA | April 22 | 8:00 pm

Sunset on Alcatraz.

Tomorrow is a new day

Yesterday, today, tomorrow.

It's going to be a beautiful evening.
One by one, the lights of the town come on.
They are reflected in the calm waters of the rivers.
The bridges light up in their turn.

The countryside quietly follows suit.
Here a street lamp and there a window that pierces the darkness of night
with its shining light.

Grids of light are proof of our presence everywhere on earth.

Night soon falls, revealing its star-studded sky.
We feel it brings hope.
We want to search for good omens in this heavenly display.

Mother Nature surrounds us, heavily laden with her gifts.
She is our ally and our companion.
Fragrant perfumes rise from the actively fertile earth.
Springtime is nigh.
It is the promise of rebirth.

The hours tick by. You turn the page. You start anew.
The sun will soon rise on a new day.
The world goes forward and our plans won't wait.

Somewhere in between Utopia, dream and reality, there is always room
for improvement.
Because life is a challenge and we want to believe in the best to come.

Elna Ragnarsdottir 📍 Borgarnes | Iceland | 10:00 pm

Petey Tina McKenna 📍 Poughkeepsie, New York | USA | March 14 | 12:00 am

Bailey Nicholle Hart 📍 Las Vegas, Nevada | USA | April 13 | 7:31 pm

Mark Bowling 📍 Shanghai | China | April 27 | 6:34 pm

Jack Brown 📍 Houston, Texas | USA | April 18 | 8:01 pm

Enrico Bruscia 📍 Milan | Italy | April 22 | 10:30 pm

Getting through a terrible time here, but we'll make it ! A view over the silent Milan.

Flavia Kaba 📍 Tirana | Albania | April 18 | 9:55 pm

Florence Pohl 📍 Brussels | Belgium | March 17 | 7:07 pm

Yoshio Tahara ♥ Tokyo | Japan | April 23 | 11:15 pm

Laura Majors 📍 Denver, Colorado | USA | April 23 | 7:56 pm

Nikola Gledic 📍 Kotor | Montenegro | April 1 | 6:39 pm

Stephen Vincent 📍 Los Angeles, California | USA | April 14 | 5:00 am

Rafael Reis 📍 Denver, Colorado | USA | April 16 | 9:38 pm

Fabio Attilio Dri 📍 Sydney, New South Wales | Australia | March 10 | 6:05 pm

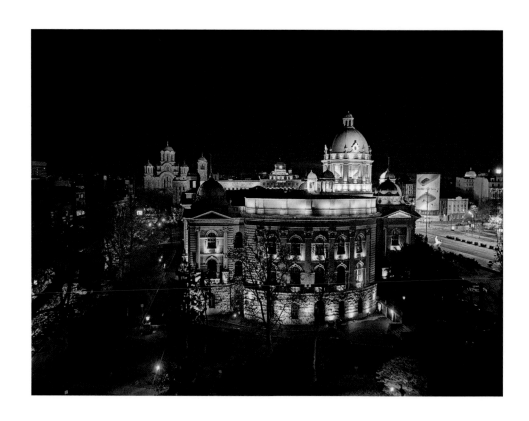

Petar Subotin 📍 Belgrade | Serbia | April 17 | 2:34 am

Philippe Chiwy 📍 Brussels | Belgium | April 9 | 11:53 pm

Gilberto Mesquita 📍 Rio de Janeiro | Brazil | April 24 | 6:01 pm

Just after Sunset with the Waxing Crescent Moon and Venus on the right side of the picture, almost aligned with the little church on the top of the hill.

Dina Zardaryan 📍 Moscow | Russia | April 25 | 7:35 pm

After the storm ends, the sun will shine... Stay safe, everyone.

Extras

Mimi Chou ♥ Oakton, Virginia | USA | March 23 | 4:35 pm

My little girl is inspired and painting the amazing views from *View from my window* to raise money to purchase lunches for you amazing front line heroes and support the small local businesses. Thank you all. Stay healthy and stay positive!

This photo wasn't in keeping with the group's rules and so we couldn't approve it. However, the story behind it deserves a special mention in this book.

The team

Administrators or moderators, all volunteers. Here are all those people who put in so much time and effort until late into the night.

BARBARA DURIAU ANNABELLE BROUHON CASSANDRA ROSÉ CATHERINE DURIAU CHRISTINA LEGRAND

CYNTHIA LEGRAND FANNY NOËL GEORGANNE DURON INGRID RUBBENS KATIA BARAN

KATJA WERBROUCK LEILA PIROT LILI CERCKEL LUCIE CENSINI ROMAN PIROT

SARAH ALTENLOH SHERON WECHSLER SO BROUHON SONJA LEGRAND VAN DIEDRICH

VINCIANE PIERART VIRGINIE DODÉMONT YANNIC TOSSINS

Members

Here are the authors of the photos illustrating this book. These are all the people who believed in me.

MAY AGIUS GUIDO ALLEVA MATISSE ANDERSEN MERJA ANTTILA CHIARA ARCADIPANE JANINE ARLIDGE MICHELE ARSENAULT HELEN ATHERTON JENNIFER AUNGELIQUE PATRÍCIA AZEVEDO NEVOA GAETANO BALESTRA LONNEKE BANK JÓHANNA BÁRA HALLGRÍMSDÓTTIR KATE BARKER ENRICO BARONE MATTIA BASEGGIO MARIA BIRNAURE TARA BISOGNA OANA BOGDAN MOLLY BOHMAN MIKE BOIVIN GEE SOO BOO STACEY BOOTH PASCALE BOURCIER MARK BOWLING KATE BRINGARDNER JACK BROWN ENRICO BRUSCIA DONNA BRYANT MEGAN BUCKLEY SHANNON CANNINGS HOWARD CARBONE CAMILA CERETTA ESMERALDO CHIODINI NETO PHILIPPE CHIWY MIMI CHOU KINTA CHUC JENNY CLARK STEPHANIE CLARKE DOROTHY COLBY GINA COOPER BERTHE COPPIN BALAZS CSERNE LEANNE CUMMINS LAUREN CUNNINGHAM ISABELLE CYR TOM DE CONINCK ELS DE HAAS SÉBASTIEN DECAMPS TERI DEMPSKI GIUSEPPINA DI NARDO BETY DIMANT BARKASZI DÓRA JANICE DOWDESWELL FABIO ATTILIO DRI MARCELA DRUMM AJOY EDWARDS KRISTÍN EINARSDÓTTIR MADELEINE ENO MIKE ESCOBER CLAIRE EVANS MICHELA FABBRI SHENA FAIRLESS SABRINA FALL LÉO FAVREAU SHELLEY FINCH COREENA FLETCHER IRENE FORCELLA GRAHAM FORD LUCILENE FRAGA KRISTIN FREED FANNY FUR-COTONEA PEARL GALBRAITH THERESA GALL FERNANDO GARCÍA-BASTIDAS JACQUELINE GARELLICK TIA GAVIN YOSARA GEERLINGS NIKOLAS GIAKOUMIDIS FANI GIALAMA PATRICIA GILLIGAN NIKOLA GLEDIC JEANNETTE GORY PAMELA GRANT NANCY GRAY JULES GRIFFITH LARS-ANDERS GRONEWOLD ANGELA GUALANDUZZI CYNTHIA GUTIERREZ-WHITE BJØRG ELIN HÅKEGÅRD JAKOBSEN MANDY HALSE WENDY HAMILTON JOHANNA HANDLEY ROBIN HARRISON BAILEY HART MARINA HAYES GRIFFEN HERRERA THOMAS HERRMANN SIRKKU HÖLTTÄ JOANNE HOOPES SHIREL HOROVITZ AURÉLIE HOX HELEN HUITINK RACHEL IRELAND EYAL IZHAR STEVE JAKOBS JANE PANDORA DIANE JHUECK TALY JOHNSON RIKKI JONES ALIZÉE JOUFFROY TIFFANY JUMP FLAVIA KABA CAROL KAFTON TOSHIKO KAMO ESTHER KASSOVICZ KAISA KAUPPINEN KERRY KENNEDY VIKTOR KESSLER GLENN KINCAID COLLEEN KISSINGER KIMMERNAQ KJELDSEN KIM KLEIN LEENA KLOSSNER ADELA KOCMAN LILA KUMAR KATH LAFFERTY JOANNE LANDFAIR PATRICK LE DEZ ALEXANDRA LEE COLA CARMEN LEGUIA SHELLEY LEWIS YILIN LIM MONICA LINDQVIST STACY LOWE CHRISTINE LUCAS LAURA MAJORS MARIE-CATHERINE MARS JOY MASSON MASAKO MATSUMOTO STEPHEN MCDOWEL PAIGE MCGOWAN STUART MCKELVIE CHRISTIANE MCKENNA JANET MCPHERSON JUAN MEJIA DOLLI MELAINE ARIANNA MEREU GILBERTO MESQUITA DEON MEYER KIRA MILAS GISELA MILMAN KIMBERLY MINER MARK MINKEVITCH SHEFALI MITRA JILL MOHRY PETER MORGAN SKY MUHAMMAD ONEIDA MURPHY SANDESH NAIDOO SHUSHANIK NERSESYAN ERNESTO NETO LUCY NEYLAN NADEZDA NEZVANOVA CAROLINE O'BRIEN MARIE OKAZAKI LUCA PACCHIONI MARIA PARISI MICAELA PAVONCELLO ISA PEERSMAN ANNE PFLIMLIN VICTORIA PICCONE LESLIE PIERCE FLORENCE POHL GABRIELLA PORCU MANUELA PORCU JONNA POULSEN RACHEL QUEINNEC SUSAN RABE SABINA RAGAINI ELNA RAGNARSDOTTIR ZRINKA RAGUŽ MINNA RAJALIN-KÄKÖNEN BERND RATHJEN LAURA REID RAFAEL REIS MANUELA RESTAGNO MICHAEL RHYS SHANTEL RICH MISTY RIGDON EUGIN ROBINSON MIMI ROBINTON MICHELLE RODIGER WALTER RODRIGUES DEBBIE RODRIGUEZ KJELL-ERIK RUUD INCO SAITO MARISTELA SALVATORI ELEKTRA SAMOILI NECLA SARIKAYA MARIA SCARVALONE LEA SCHMELING TERRY SCHWARTZ LILLIAN SCOLES NATLINA SENGMANY KESTELL SERFONTEIN ASYA SERGEEVA TANIA SHAH MANISHA SHAH HOLLY SHEPHERD TONYA SIDOTI BETH SIGHTLER SIWLA SILVA ELIZABETH SIMPSON TIMOTHY SINAGUGLIA PETER SINKOVICS EVGENY SLOBODSKI MELANIE SMITH ELIZABETH SMITH ALEXA SOKOL SUE SOUTOR SUSAN SPEED SUE STANFORD CHRISTY STEWART PETAR SUBOTIN MARIANNE SUNDE HESTETUN TAMMY SWITZER YOSHIO TAHARA STÉPHANIE TAILLANDIER KATHRYN TAYLOR RYAN TERPSTRA JULIE THALER NGHI TRAM MARIA TRAN EVA TRUBETSKAYA JUDIT TUNA MICHEL VAEREWIJCK INGRID VAN DEN BOOGAARD GEERT VAN KAATHOVEN PATRICIA VARGAS BELMONTE ANASTASIA VENETSANOU MIEKE VERKEYN ALICE VISSCHER SANDRA VIVIER IRENE LAVON WALKER LILI WAMBACHER-KRIEGELSTEIN LINDA WESTBROOK STEVEN WHITFIELD KATE WILSON REBECCA WILSON HÅKAN WIRTÉN MELISSA WISTEHUFF GARY WORNELL CHUCK WYSONG HISHAM YOUSSEF BONGA ZAMISA DINA ZARDARYAN MARGARITA ZOBNINA JENNIFER ZSÜRGER

Aknowledgments

And all of a sudden, here I am, with the feeling of being at the Oscars. The one where I could make everyone step on stage. The one where I would be wearing those precious high heels. The thing is, I can't walk in high heels. So here I am, just with my sneakers, as it's more comfortable. After all, it's just us here, isn't it?

I call up all the contributors of the crowdfunding campaign that supported this crazy project, "View From My Window - life after Facebook". It's thanks to them that you are holding this book in your hands. I cannot mention all 3,146 of them here. Thank You.

I call up my team. The ones that helped me, comforted me, stimulated me, and stopped me from going wild when it was needed. Thank You.

I call up Suzi that dragged me, quite effortlessly, to settle in Amsterdam. This town that inspired me in quite an amazing way. Thank You.

I call up my Swiss knife. He doesn't know yet I found him this nickname. He does now. Thank You, Pascal.

I call up Dominique, my friend, and the author of the texts in this book. To have let himself get criticised, be mistreated, for at the end of the day, to be appreciated. To have made me burst into laughter when some situations could have seemed actually quite dramatic. Thank You.

I call up Viviane, to have promoted this project to the Belgian press when VFMW was only a few days old. Thank You.

I call up Anna, my English teacher. She still has quite some work! Thank You.

Finally – we will need to squeeze up a bit – I call up all the members of the *View from my window* community. You that have posted, liked, commented, those millions of posts. You that have given me as many sleepless nights as these totally unexpected emotions. Thank You.

NB

Most of these photos were taken with smartphones, which explains why the quality varies from one photo to the next. As for the comments, we have kept them as they were originally published online with the aim of preserving their spontaneity.

Concept & graphic design:
Barbara Duriau

Content writer:
Dominique Maricq

Translation:
Catherine Hillman
Peter Steven
Simon John Steven

First edition

© 2020

ISBN : 978-90-830914-1-9
NUR 653

Printed in October 2020.
The BXRBXRX editions are the propriety of Barbara Duriau

" **Now I want to travel** "

- Claudia W.

Country	Value
United States	1.2 M
Australia	170,531
United Kingdom	102,576
Belgium	85,939
Canada	76,539
Brazil	64,860
South Africa	60,599
Italy	43,154
France	33,042
Israel	31,283

City	Value
New York City, USA	35,561
Sydney, Australia	34,424
Brussels, Belgium	26,768
Melbourne, Australia	25,387
Brisbane, Australia	23,966
Los Angeles, USA	21,471
São Paulo, Brazil	17,805
Perth, Australia	17,201
Budapest, Hungary	15,929
London, UK	15,731